Gifts To A Butterfly

A Collection of Poetry and Photo Art By

Carly West

Copyright © 2020, 2014 by Carly West

All rights reserved. This book or any portion thereof may not be reproduced or used in any manner whatsoever without the express written permission of the publisher except for the use of brief quotations in a book review.

All poetry, photography art, book and cover designs by Carly West.

ISBN-10: 0991457412
ISBN-13: 978-0-9914574-1-0

In Loving Memory Of
Grandpa Fred
&
My sister Cali

Butterfly

She was created to fly
Like a butterfly
A sweet thief to brush your cheeks
Leaving a sensuous kiss
Then off to see existence
But only after she undressed
And let forth her wings
To expand and to bring
Love unlike all the world

In stillness is her love
This queen of all the world
So ache no more
Open your hands
To feel the land of the butterfly
A sight to ever behold
A beauty to know of this bliss.

Press

Press her, she will flood
The brush will be enough
If you will brave it
Press her, she wants you
The need is breaking through
If you will save it

Press her as you know now
The way comes natural
When you will do it
Press her to be free
The move becomes the dream
When you will prove it

There is no reason fathomed
To hide a love unlike existence
But the soul knows it's safe haven
When its heart is finally taken

Psalm

The hunter for his hunger
Is satisfied by my eyes and only mine
The finer temptings are in my palm
And when in bed, the holy psalm
In vines called arms
In mass called body
In breath called life
Of thee.

The Hunger, The Harm

Why do you never leave me?
When you try to keep me away
Why when I thought to find freedom
I see your face

Should love be a thorn to bleed?
More than skin to the air I breathe
Will it ever end, could it?
If you can't touch me at all

Why do you always come back?
When you try to stay apart
Do you know what I tear in you?
We bear such fear

Should love be a rose on a grave?
Withered and died from passing of days
Will it ever change, could it?
If you won't touch me at all

The cold again
Did I ever know sun?
Am I forced to be
Left with a longing for warmth?
Try to touch me, here in your reach
Try to let go of what kills you with me
We will cry now
We will die within arms
Should the hunger, be seen as the harm

I cannot compete
With your stolen mind
And the walls of stone
That stay your heart in bind

Yet I love you, more than love
And I'll send above
That you will know love
One day, one day

Still...

Why is there press to my mass?
When you spoke to care
But silence my speak
I burn in the hold of a night
And then you're gone

Should love be shot in the dark?
Unseen so we know not your aim
Will it ever expose, could it?
If you don't break down at all

No matter legion of demons
To mask forth the feel of our souls
Weakened, alas, yet forbearing
Try to touch me, here in your reach
Try to say so
What kills you with me
We will cry now
We will die within arms
For this hunger, cannot be a harm

Love, I am I, divulging creature
You are you, a true endeavor
Akin below the surface
If we just touch us
If we just touch
One day.

Sacred

I am this world
Of more than love
Of more than breath
And taste for you

I am this essence
That burns you on
The strength to come
The weak to suck

I am this body
That holds me in
That becomes of you
The deep flesh connect

I bare the thunder
That roars for you
I sex seeping vines
Into every skin of you

I bare the knowledge
What shines in secret
I feast the joys and pains
All that run your veins
And throw your bones

For all to see and not see
And only you and I to know
Let weave, let rhyme, let beat
This existence of more than being
All we are, we are together
Sacred lover.

Mortal

Reign, a sounding of command
Rain, a pouring of concede
I am where I am
In the midst of a barren field
Bringing pieces into place
I set the stage for battlefield

Who leads the march behind me waits?
Who dawns the day before me wakes?
This is I, in body of
Embellished strength, praying "Dear God"
Rescue mortal from the sword
Charges onward meant to pierce

Yes, let there be amour guarding silk
Within, without a fate to brave and save
May there be Heaven again
After the Hell surrenders
And calms the mighty storm

Oh, strength is beaten
Wounds appear, the body sore
Would a scream deliver retreat
Or an army birthed of victory?
One gift bestowed from God
Deserve I? I pause but accept the will
And still have some to raise the dead
Fare thee well, forward I stand

Come nature's force in mass
Sword aimed high, shield to chest
Not brave but only in love
In truth, in hope, with blood
Oh God, I'm wounded
Eyes behold a heavy war
Over it be, although I remain
Onto the ground this body rests

The spirit heals and grows beyond
To come back to me, the better I
And breathe in life again
With newness fresh and bold
See and touch this resurrect
To know, this is who I am.

Burned

To push aside a feeling
The blind will starve to death
Should I ignore the racing
Will I suffer without breath?

To wander in the wasteland
The count of haunt goes up
Am I too late to meet you
And bathe in wine of your cup?

I never meant to hurt you
I never meant to stay away
But I burned from the flame
Needing you all along

A torture on the inside
The wait is hard to hold
Does the victim rise again
When he turns against the cold?

An angel in possession
The want beyond design
Are we free to overcome
And ascend in this alignment?

Healed by your exception
Accept me as I was
And I was saved
Because you braved
The wasteland.

Presence

Rapture found me
Where I was hiding
Walls raised around me
And still defying
Then enters a wonder
I'm exposed beyond my cover
Never to be lost

I lay inside a restless slumber
Pondering over your cold shiver
Circles endless find us present
When you request my hand

And I keep folded on the soft ground
Making traces with my fingers
In the sweet air, I feel you here
As if on my blush skin
My heart racing wild

See me running far away
See me running to this place
See me running, ever on
See me run away

And every season I return
Where you frequent my horizon
Follow footsteps in the forest
Where I find you in your bare skin
You in waiting as if knowing
I was coming
Close, and home again.

Gold Fingers

The leaving of traces
Those lingering voices
From your lips and mine
And it kills me
It stings like pretty red rose pricks
Shedding petals of colour once loved
But time as a lover
Moves on in the morn

A breath from the deep, my eyes close
In still, I see a momentous view
Then enters a stalwart
I'm weakened and fevered
He knows me too well
But only a past cast over and buried
Mourning has finally long ceased
As awaken I am now
And so present, thank God

Should it come, the stranger of you
If it's old, move along till it's new
Then I'll choose tomorrow
For today I release to the wind

And sleep till I dream
An image of a cradle
To never be broken
A pulse from a heartbeat
Hell bent in passion
The fusion of gods
For my fingers are gold.

You Are

I'm caged to be released
I chased the beast away
I've been beaten to the core
But there's no sore in wounds

In time resides the quiet
In truth adorns the freedom
In prayer begets the answers
In love beckons the only reed

To be full of what I need
I've never seen in anyone
A wish became the realness of you
The missing is no more

You are to be discovered
I am to be delivered
Beating hearts are raced to death
You are to be desired
I am to be devoured
Our bodies hot and out of breath

In time I taste the quiet
In truth we'll always be
My prayer is said for you
In love, in love we are
Because you are the beauty.

Mortality

Laid to rest is my love
On the bed once made sacred
In a wake that did not exist

Upon this day
Upon this very day
I surrender body and soul
For in this hour
I'm sailed into my end
The cruel taunt of time and space

Loss begat a dire strain
No room for the moonlight of hope
For gone from me
Gone from me, alas
Was the strength of armies
Burned in fire, shield and sword

Faith once had my brave
A stalwart spanning miles
For unbelieved was I
At tear, to break
The mold of firm and fair
Hell begged to find my heel

Into a grave I fell
The hands of mind lost in labyrinth
For darkness closed
Darkness felt around
To blanket in layer as skin
From depth prayed I mercy

No one came for days
Though I was not alone
I swear it by my very life
This had reason to be the sleep

I'd wake not from
The mind of man would deem so true
But hell does not mind man
Therefore, I pressed

Pressed on to spare my life
Where purpose hides in mortality
For must it be vain
Must it be in vain
Birth with no noble reasons
If only to know the unknown

What breath still waits to pass?
From somewhere under laden surface
Silence reigned a gift
I began to rise from a death end
No man can express as I levitated
Far away from me

And touching my body revealed
A like form to that I once knew
Yet how it feels exotic, so exotic
When glancing a shed of skin behind
Holy be, I am moved with no define

Now upon ground to take rest
There remained a pulse within chest
For here I lay bare
Lay with no care to leave
The solitude that beds me now
Oh, warmth given to my closed eyes

What follows, know I not
This moment feels, hollow and fatigued
But should love resurrect, in oath I give
I will protect it, I will.

In Between

Window mirrors candlelight
Longing out into the mist
And your wishes
Tantalized by colour
Set the flame

When you know
What I haven't found
I won't resist at all
I won't force a strain

Undressed for now
And see me later
And write such letters
Declaring intricates
You find secret in me

Ask the words
I'll never not search
For something beautiful
Consuming, I consume

Set a body free
Let the spirit freeze in time
Forgotten love changes us
You and I, love alive
And nothing in between.

Love Be

He:
From weathered eyes
Her being cannot be denied
Beneath her breasts
Her mane to heel is gorgeousness
I cannot rest her linger
Aching to touch with every finger
The orgasmic mass
Engulfed in every attract
God, she is thine
She is mine, my angel

She:
He wrote to my body, heart, and mind
Every inch of my racing to entwine
In this be it true
His confess coming through
Love, be it love, now a loud

He:
From gathered miles
Her generous saved mine inside
Because her grace
Out of hell I elevated
I cannot rest in sleep
Hungering ours to be freed
The levelous whole
Marveled this soul
God, she is thine
In her own, my angel

She:
He writes to my thin, thick, and alone
Every inch of my skin, blood, and bone
God, be this true
His connect coming through
Love, be it love, now a loud

He:
From beneath moves
It was hell to be removed from you
In silent refrains
Held still the love in pains
I cannot rest in romance
No one is she, no one will match
The glorious love
Defined pass love and trust
God, she is thine
Hers and mine, Earth angel

She:
He repents to us, requests for us
Every part of the two into one
Oh God, blessed truth
Our exalt shining through
Love, be it love, now a loud

Us:
With all that I am to you
Yes, with all I am to you
Dear woman, you amaze
Gentleman, you engage
You fill in my dreams
You fill in my means
I hunger in breathing
I thunder in breathing
How it seems
Always seems
That we feel
That we feel
In forever.

Promise

I promise to crawl the floor
I promise to cry till no breath
I promise to faint till death
And melt into the maze

Beginnings are when ends have been
Words never found will be caught & said
And into the depths of eternity
We will fade, we will fade

I promise to give my skin
I promise to drain every vein
I promise to cross bodied soul
And melt into the daze

Engaging the light to morph the dark
And moves encourage the will to let love
And into the reach of entity
We will fade, we will fade

So I promise to leave no room
I promise to burn out the fight
I promise to taste my waste of you
And melt into the haze

May legions of beings surround
So loving to protect our light
If every thought surrenders to heart
And you stay in me well pass this night

I can see we will fade
I can believe we fade
By the promise
The promise we make whole.

The Revealing

A King's speech
You breathed into me
With a mouth
With a body
In a warm night
In a warm blush
Nothing could hush this design
As we cried

A queen's touch
I pressed into you
With eyes
With a body
On a hot bed
On a heated rush
Nothing could hush this design
As we cried

More than want, more than need
Feed the fire, no lust or greed
Only passion be, in humanity wear
Moved to push, moved to pull
Full of fire, a pool to drown
Into passion flee, in humanity fair

The turn so fleeting
We couldn't resist
From dusk till dawn
The ravishing strong
Enough to taste of heaven
In here and now

The yearn so waking
We couldn't deny
Come morning light
The revealing kind
Enough to break of heaven
In here and now

Yet through our eyes slight clouded fear
A thought to lose stares in the mirror
The head bows down, there is no sound
Floating from what we became

I meet your gaze
You look away
But take my hand
And kiss my face
You leaving now, another time
Oh God, to fight the fight

And so the nights turn to dark
And everyday finds no light
In the silence, in the wait

A royal cross
We live out the cost
With a heart
With a body
To a broken miss
To a broken promise
Nothing could hush this design

As we cried
As I died, never the same
As you died, no return again
How we cried
God, we cried
This King and Queen.

Clutched

The reach attacks us both
Clutched to no let go
I am inside your pain
Behind names, a palace
Sure in safety and depth
The definition of mine and thine
So heart, lay calm
I be you soon
To live, to love, to consume.

Redeemed

Oh God, love was
I panicked in the dark
Such air in thick
A weight upon my breast
I shivered every night
Warmth was gone
With no fire to heat
And love cried like helpless to death
Eyes closed on fading wishes

A demon captured
An angel who was free
But love, it was love
To redeem my folly
God, Love
I've forgiven the feast
Drawn the line straight
With no high rise falling
Knowing now, whether I stay or go
I turn the key and see
The light agrees.

Fired

I raged a choir
Let thunder sting as ashes fly
Let burn the sky every rise in me
For you see, I found love
Buried in my know

As I live and breathe
And from this day
The way I wake has changed
More than a smile or a touch
Is the feeling of being
Fired from the inside
And to deny would be to die
Before the journey ends

I raged a choir
Let lightning quake the earth
Let arrows fly and rain the sky
From every wise in me
For you see, I found love
Buried in my soul

As I live and breathe
And from my mouth
The words I say have changed
More than a phrase, more than a speech
It's being fired from inside
And to hide would be to lie
Before the sun ascends

Yes, I raged a choir
It knows no fear
And from this single tear
It shall be heard
It shall be known
Truth, my love, lives here.

True Blood

Some mind field abyss
The cold and the mist, deceive me
The fall on a sword
The broke lovers cord, released me
The missing of sun wakes of the night
No moon to cast a glow
Still I see all around
But my own I don't know
Blind as born with no eyes

Numb is the tide
Overplays does my mind
Fights in my fair to keep peace
And uncover pass years
A long love no spear can reach
When the only rescuer is I

Cries of pale in true blood
The veins sail far into warm dawns
Flowing beyond the captain to my soul
Through wind, storm, and rain
The vision retains
Slightly clouded in kind
Such sadness but no anger
The face fades to a stranger
With eyes to stir my crown

Some god-filled amends
The blunt and the bends, relieve me
The death to be born
When caused to adorn, unleash me
A virgin but wise
The new skin with shine
Dimensional vast, something to last
And it shall last me
Into forever and more.

Ivy Satin

I have silence
Thick in my chest
Cannot recall having breath
But I envision it
Something of a wind
Chanting memories
Flowing so blissful

And pure in repent
I've spent this day heavy
Hearted and seeking refuge
A refugee I might be
But I smile
Too much for it to claim
The prize of envy
Like ivy satin
Wearing on the skin
In hardly nothing

For the rest of dress
I long for to be his touch
Of no resist in a lifetime
And maybe I'll love him
Perhaps a bit less
Or as much as he
But that's only a dream
Because you see
I cannot breathe.

The Road

To suffer in hope
Is the deepest throw
Beyond the heaviest sea
To the ends the eyes
Both body and spirit
Cannot see, cannot mean

To suffer in hope
Is the saddest rose
Beyond the most striking thorn
Pass the ends of feel
Both body and spirit
Cannot please, cannot core

To suffer in hope
Is the longest wait
Beyond the racing hands
And the ends in time
Both body and spirit
Cannot say, cannot man

To suffer in hope
Is the darkest cage
Beyond the thickest steel
Like the ends that bind
Both body and spirit
Cannot bend, nor unwield

To suffer in hope
Is the cruelest brave
Beyond the strongest wish
As the ends combined
Both body and spirit
Cannot fight, nor resist

To suffer in hope
Pray you never know
To suffer in hope
The dying seeds sown
To suffer in hope
Is the heights never shown

And yet...

Is the road through your soul
Leads to reveal of vast unknowns
Is what gave, no one else could give
To me, to me, to my own
The gift to breathe
The light to live
To live and breathe
In these oceans.

Beauty Marks

For under your mask I found you
Hiding as a thief in the night
Without a reason to harm
Only holding back what is your aim

For do you love?
And do you long to understand?
All the beads in the hourglass?
And the writing on your palm?

The calm divide of fortitude
God grant my just one wish
As I take your lips in clutch
Did you ever think to be so bold?

I see it is you, the enemy
Who tosses the cares you implore
Tis true we've known us before
But if you run, the dark devours the light

Stare in my eyes, you pretty thing
Let me sex the fear from you
Let all the times of wrong undo
As a free man, released and breathed

Give to me your hand
Let me trace what is your curves
Of lines and of beauty marks
This map of the buried heart.

Dimensions

If into your body I enter
Will your soul set free
And reveal completely
Everything about you
I feel endlessly
Want as much as need

If into your body I enter
Will beyond love, we become one?

If into your mind I wander
Will your spirit unveil
And divulge completely
Every thought inside you
I hear endlessly
Want as much as need

If into your mind I wander
Will beyond trust, we become one?

To side you, not guide you
To give and receive
To be you, not own you
To know and conceive
Call you the means of creation

Bewitched and bewildered
Fails far in respect
Enhanced and embedded
Hails to sacredness
Call you the keen of creation

Grant me to thy chamber
To live and to breathe
Never I be a stranger

For without you, I grieve
Calling the deep of creation

Into your body and mind
Undressing your spirit
Attaining full combine
Leaving the world and tasting nirvana
As the truth rushes out of me

The value of heaven levitates me
Into your body and mind
Of the journey so sweet
The destination so kind

If into your soul I anchor
Will your essence unite
And embody completely
Every reach within you
I know endlessly
Want as much as need

If into your soul I anchor
Will beyond touch, we become one?

Now enter me in you
Now enter you in I
A time of ascension
Into godly dimensions
Suspended in space till we grace us

Come swiftly, my cradle
My kingdom, my throne
Say so I may enter
Your body, mind, and soul
Do grant me home.

Beware

Who would never do
And break down for you?
I'm not one to parade
Unwound for you

Lady in slumber
Lady could never sleep
Alone at night, in fight
I'm not the same
I'm not for the take
Holding in tight
And swearing off the night

A dance with beauty agrees with me
If done by qualified reach
For days are long in ecstasy
When your fill is taken in care
But when I dress within your care
Hear this now
Beware.

Bit

When in walk
The melancholy's sweet
Tasting more than burned my tongue
For you bit into me
As if I was ripe
And only for you
Therefore, I conclude in demise
To my stubborn fuel
Well, you were right.

Mistake

The grave mistake
Never played out but in my mind
Leaving was no impasse
For the eyes held the anger
Felt but not said aloud
How deafening to fragile ears

Yet my last attempt
Cried free of my twisted tongue
Before praying a quick return
There was no other way to break it

And once it begins to end
Nothing prevents the follow
Free from everything cannot be
Regardless of wills to sever
These hands are weak
Yet stretch forth to say
What will not be said here tonight

Now pull out the string that ties
The rope binding us still
Look away and cut it fast
We're going to stop this with a truce
Wrap your end around your finger
Let this remind you, in truth, I'm loose

No crying offers of apologies
Crawling with bruised knees
Bring relief to cease the burden
And give to us our freedom
This string of our truce
Make it tight till you build blood
Let this remind and bind you, I'm loose

Oh, the grave mistake
Never played out but in my mind
There was no other way to break it.

Four

Four times the phone will ring
One believing you are there
Two and three filled with hope
The last one just in case
Then I'll hang up
And think to do again later, or not
If you don't answer
You'll never hear what I need to say

Four times I scream your name
One believing you will come
Two and three filled with fear
The last one just in case
Then I'll give up
Dream of you once again, or not
If you don't answer
I'll never sleep with you in mind

Four times I'll plead sorry
One believing you'll believe
Two and three filled with defeat
The last one just in case
Then I'll break up
And surrender your things, I will
If you don't answer
Too much will be left to remain unsaid

I can see you trying to get back to me
I can see you trying to get back at me

But four times I'll say goodbye
One because I mean it
Two and three to remind you
The last one to close up
Then I'll end it
And burn to you this letter after
I will, God, I will
For the four times you don't answer.

Next

A fire sips the air
Are you the form in flame?
Rebels point to you
But I protest lost love
I don't brave the coward

Sun to rain to hell again
Here's something for a scent of lust
More of less there's no protest
You must have moved the motion on
To the next one

So strange
The color of dancing danger
Collapsing over me
So strangers
The two have turned out to be
Forgive my failing mind.

Parlay

Use not a knife but a stake
Send it deep until it shakes
And I wake up to heaven
A vision I had no imagining
Of all I ache for in my soul
All kept beholden by hope

Though if you seep, I will rise
Never to look back
And never to think twice
But love my sin.

In Sleep

Like a fool stranded blind
Like a time you once forgot
Like a sting that leaves a scar
Like a target easy to spot

The way more leaves me less
The words lost I cannot say
The days drawn without colour
The feel I received in pain

More smiles to the dark
More fever enhancing chills
Tears when gone is nowhere
My strength drained from lost will

As you lived in me
How to overcome and break through
I chose to be again
I chose to breathe again

Distance could be the safest kept
But memories get the less of me
When visions of you
Run through the soul you've crept into

Now I'm screaming in my sleep
I open my eyes
And keep seeing you everywhere
Why must it be this way?

Like a fool stranded blind
I have to be again
Oh God, I have to live again.

Heart Fare

Goodbye is a hard road to fathom
After revealed a love that once was
We say why now
For a moment so fleeting
When all we've known
Is what's meant to be
As much as it pulls me
It's not for us to be
And I cannot be here anymore

This feels like some passionate warfare
Exotic to the heart but toxic to taste
You've been a strong force to me
Broke down walls I held so close
But I know we must walk away
If I could be in two places
Would that make us happy?
Heaven says we'll be just fine

You keep looking at me this way
And I keep stopping then starting
I'm pulling apart my heart
It will not be what we want it to be
When our hearts hit the deep end
God give us the strength
To do what we have to
We cannot be torn in two
Oh, we cannot be torn in two

Night has come, we're both in silence
Standing skin to skin and pushing
Steps behind till we're out of light
Because we know, in releasing hold
It's not our time.

Madness

Then into hell I climbed
Like the madness of a mother
Into torture and pain
For the safety of my lover

And how I found my heart
Beating for our being
And how he held me in
Only angel eyes believing
In love more than all of life

Tell the world
There will never be another
What was Heaven sent
Transcends above the cover
Of skin and blood, bones and crust

I've bled beyond all romance
Unseen by anyone
But this wonderous love
Began by a striking glance

Tell the world
So they may witness this
As these unearthly touches
Transcend above the cover
Of skin and blood, bones and lust

I've reached beyond all circumstance
Unknown to anyone
For I am, wonderous love
Began by a godly hand.

Dark & Light

Upon the chest scribe thy wish
Into the womb share thy secret
And to the crown
Oh, mighty crown
Place thy dream
Sweet visions conceived
In the dark, in the light, in between

If ever we believed
Let it be this
A slow dance at dusk
Lasting on, coming on
Till the morn

Thy moves cover me
I bask in such flavor
When give and receive glow the light
To bond the souls
Should I weep, then weep with me
Through the night
And every night
In the dark, in the light, in between

Vibrant blues burn into essence
Inhale each bliss as the roses meet
Again and again
Deeper than the deep
And resist nothing
It's all encompassing
Thy live of breath to mine

If ever we rekindle
A supernova preceding stars
How vast in enchantment
The smallest shines for all of this
Amongst the bliss
Between the two to one
Come love, come love
Define us

Wear us thick and thin resist
Only safety here
Only here in the clutch
Of the dark, of the light, in between.

Sword

Hunching to the rain
The skin grows damp within
Surrounded by my thoughts
I stop and weep
I dared not understand
The beauty pushed and pulled
Befriended by my ghosts
I cannot speak
Mesmerizing glances
Been wandered far too long
Much deceived by my weakness
I plead for home

East to west drew time and space
Fractured by my fear, I lied and hid
From the dancing of a siren
Blazing through, around my heart
Overcome and overwhelmed
I threw my sword down
Screaming love in every inch of me
Overcome and overwhelmed
I raised my shield up and tasted blood

Warming from the sun
The haunting dies away
Infused by truth, unharmed
I drop and breathe
Forgiveness protects when pain
Salvation by my lover, in might
I pray forever

I'll stop at nothing to redeem
Come the storms and plaguing seas
I'll eat of life and devour death
If you'll always be my breath
I need the need
I'll be bold in vulnerability
For through it all and still remains
I know we're meant to be in love.

Between Legs

When on my chest, repress
Remind the mind to heart
And the heart to free
The stings of wounds
And let the dawn seep in
As a beautiful kiss
And sin between my legs

To melt away in lanes of love
Such flames I made
But none took in
For the burn could eat me dead
Yet to die for the cause of touch
I shall unveil the core of my fill
And never regret us

In fall, decide I to fall
The wild horse bows down
To gifts of you
The bares of nakedness
And the race of a stallion
With a sensuous reach
And me in his eyes

How can I tremble?
A force flooding body, turns in
And when you shake with me
It's more than beauty
And lost from my words
For the sake of inhale
Let us yearn

For sunrise in your mass
A view of dramatic reveal
I'm overcome and overwhelmed
By what we've designed
And in the warmth of sun
You were right, so right
As now in throws we have won.

Oxygen

Madness ran the river
Where we feared to tread
When I went to wade
I was left for dead
Further from horizon
Of love and ecstacy
Pulling need and greed
Of a beast no longer weak

Flooded of waves
Is it wrong to crave safety?
As my body floats the course
I struggle to find will
To say and scream exhaust
So tired of the cost of time
And crossed by bridges burned

I never yearned for anything
The way I do for oxygen
Give a fresh into our love
And ease the taste of blood
The redness of our lips
The way I feel I've sinned
Distant was this skin
Hope worn thin and pale

If once to know the night
Of we a lover together
I leave it be to eternity
And bite my tongue at never
Though sore as love has seen
I must sacred this to all end
When your heart once lived its make
You know it will come again

As we sleep
As we dream
And live
We will be.

Novas

If eternal burns a naked flame
Crawl through hell, scream my name
Reach with thunder, make the rain
Hunt me down with no restraint

Calling fever to rise again
Heated flavor must be shed
As blood to veins our bodies' bed
Love come, love come
Speak, I've said

Death became her
Only to be who I am
Death became him
As the man who burns as I

When darkness draws a breathless need
Expel your inhale, breathe in me
Clutch with passion, no space between
Ravish whole, receive, conceive

Novas bracing to deep explode
Owning deepness, eating the bones
As voice to throat, our bodies moan
Love come, love come
Strong, enthrone

Life became her
Now I stand again
Life became him
As the friend best in my deep.

Sword & Bow

The haunt of my heart
Such a stone amen
An omen of storms in heave
The faint as it comes
Hums softly in blood
I can hear the suck of my breath
And the tone of my lips as they form a kiss
Out to the ethereal of you

For I am in pulsation
Of elation of eloquent rush
With a weakness for touch
In longing too much
In possession that questions revere
So severe are the wounds
To move bleeds the two
But surely the battlefield clears

When the look, smell, savor of love
Out sounds the raging of canons
No soldiers but warriors
Neglecting let go in seclude
Where lovers in hue merge skin, fare & air
Lifted to dimensions created

The haunt of my heart
Seductive in whispers
Mirages the smoky night stare
The war as it was
Burned all but the crust
Quivers to rob us the silence
But I repel every violence of us

Down your sword, down my bow
Come the rain flow to die
The fires that claim life and soul
Each to be so devoted
Each to give up our lives
Not to take, nor to break
But to save the glory of the love.

God's Arms

The colour of my blood
Never before was named
A maze among my veins
Racing in paces irreverent
You made me boil, the fiercest flame
You made me coil
At the force of my desire

Wander as a stranger
Lost for days ate by nights
Waited till the time had ripened
And come you did, to collect

Me from the graves
Me from the waste in deep
Me from the flesh fade
Me to the arms of gods

The colour of your blood
Never before was shed
A river denied the flow
Bracing in faces irreverent
I made you weak, the concrete tame
I made you speak
Words with silence burning

Wander as a danger
Crossed for days ate by nights
Waited till the time had broken
And come you did, to resurrect

Me from the waves
Me from the waste of need
Me from the flesh tear
Me to the arms of gods

Saw into your bare
And I was born by breath again
As what was sonant from your mouth
I was found and loved.

Breathless

I cannot breathe
If I cannot breathe
How can I tell you
I love you

I cannot move
If I cannot move
How can you and I
Dance the light

Do you see it in my eyes?
Does it feel within my kiss?
Does the touch express such feel?
In realness all too real

I love so much it aches
An ache so deep to cry
Ask of me, for the change in us
Has moved the seas of love

And I cannot dream
If I cannot dream such greater
I know this is it
In the all I could say
I live thee.

Awake

Laid down and loved
Wounded, we are mended
And on bended knee
You beseech of me
Into the dawn a raging seed
And I am made silent
Overrun of drowning eyes
Erased from pain
We are awake
And in love for love
We will reign

Laid down and loved
Open, we are in receive
Of all the depths we ran
Away, now holding strong
Into the dawn with insatiable need
And you are made silent
Overrun of loss of breath
Erased from shame
We are awake
And in love for love
We saturate

Laid down and loved
Godly in this hour
And all the days and nights
To come when does the sun
You are in me as my blood
Rushed by every touch
Eye to eye, no move of the tongue
Awake and in love for love.

Do

In anything I'd do
I'd do anything for you
As I'd do this for myself
In life, in death, in joy, in pain

You are a fire
Constant flaming in my soul
You are a breath
So many, adding to my whole

And now you know out loud
It joins the know within
It's pure and sin
A thirst, a need, a wish
So kiss me, or miss me

Would anything you do
Be done as anything for me
As you'd do for yourself
In life, in death, in joy, in pain

Say I'm a rage
Violent passion in your soul
Say I'm an ocean
Surely endless, beauty overflown

Oh, let me know out loud
To join this hope within
It's pure and sin
Hunger, thunder, the wish
So kiss me, kiss me complete
Or you'll miss me.

Beast

See there now, be slow
Queen Goddess, come away
To feel in close
Her love found true
Buried within her breast

To force the thieves of battles
Out danced a brave, a mighty marvel
To witness views
Monsters found bled
Slain because her resonance

Dear sun, blind us
Dear God, remind us
To own the beauty
And kill the beast

Can we know then, what rages
Repeat strikes derail the course
But Heaven protects the gold
Never to wear that radiant skin
But decided by her hold

Dear Earth, ground us
Dear God, abound us
To love the beauty
But kill the beast

Do not feast here, beast
Go on, meet your maker
For now we take her and follow through
For now we love us and kill you.

You Don't

Some relative moments
Fell away in desperation
What's so mad tonight?
Some cut lines between
And a throw of burning words
I would never mean for you

Lonesome defines these fences
When I fight to settle in
Into nothing more without you
I fight it now again
It tears the heart apart
But you don't look away

All these minute offerings
Holding in some fierce desire
Does not let you see
One bad act repeats
Until I'm done and defeated
By truth, by you

Lonesome is not sadness
When I get to picture you
Reaching, seeing all my feelings
You're felt at every turn
It tears the heart apart, my heart
But you don't look away

When I try to reach through
All the things I meant to say
My last mistake
But I do what I can to show
I'm always on your side

Your heart apart, your heart apart
But you don't look away
This heart apart, this heart apart
With everything to say
What's so mad tonight?

Scarlet

Scarlet rose
Claim your victim's heart
Seduce with insatiable scent
The way to lasting passion

It's me you chose
I beg your mercy
This chance to offer you
The freedom of my love

Scarlet rose
Push away the wait
My eyes close so tight
Doubt stirs heavy within

It's me that's thrown
I ask the question
For the way to believe
In the gift of love

But will you hurt me
Will you cut me with your thorns?
I stand so cautious
Yet look to seize your refuge

Oh, hear me thunderous night
Bring silence to an instinctive need
It's growing full and thirsting to feed
On the one who be the given soul
To calm the untamed sea
I only pray it's you
Tonight, it has to be you

Oh, Scarlet rose
I'm bleeding now
The ache has overtaken
But I'm still open
Needing your life in me
Somehow.

Explode

In a siege, but in surprise
I give no fight, I give in
Hell at brink too long
I did not win
So lock the chains
The vicious rain
Can drown me now

My mirage creates
A weakened bridge to love
I've wandered cold
Pushed from every open door
And a store of roses
I cannot keep
For they would bleed me dead

But today, be my death
Cause a smile sly
When release from detriment
Is the thought of joy
My soul could so expose
And explode to never know
No more sorrow.

Eating

Suck in
I do, a breath
Of air so fresh, I drown
It's freeing and flying
The oldness is dying down
The permanent sunset to color
Some savor and hunger alive
I open my mouth
And so goes my mind
To flavor of eating life.

Dust

Rome hast died
I've shed no further cares
You are left to cry alone
Rome hast died
And no longer will it stand
You are left to dense ruins

Do you hear it has died?
So beautiful, and dear Lord, she tried
Apart from the heart where it crashed
As all came tumbling to the old ground
The sound made angels cry

My beloved fair
The glare of rain drowns me here
For there is no more
But stings to kiss me now
Beside my fortress
She flames to fly away

Stone to dust
Glass to shattered diamonds
But it shall not matter till tomorrow
When the loss does chill the soul
And no substance bears thee hold

My disdain of cowardice
And your distress of fortune
Traverse the common flow
To stunning with my attendance
Pained by your cunning
As such charm slips out of view
For my survival

Rome, you leave me now
My chariot awaits
The clouds disperse to daylight
And I bury you
The Earth shall eat your stones
I wear the weight no more

Old Rome has died
Old Rome has died
Old Rome has died
So she may never cry again.

Beautifully Plagued

*So beautifully plagued
Coming undone
At the thought of your hands*

*Respectfully yours
In the words of a friend
A close moment repeats
In the scenes of my head*

*So beautifully plagued
What's deemed right and wrong
How do I begin to define?*

*Selectively drawn out
More than my face from a crowd
And ponder simple meanings
When everything takes shape*

*Without moving your lips
Whisper the words
And request my hand
As the world slows down for us
There is only one step to love*

*As it calls us into seclude
The intrigue of our beguile
Curse the night without the flesh
For you said you love
When coming undone.*

Eyes

In my own eyes
Storms cannot succeed
In my own eyes
Taste the sighs of relief
I tell you I'm ready
I'll tell you
I'll show you my weakness
As you burn in my strength

Pleaded and hunted
Calm and designed
Fearful in trembles
Angels in eyes

In your lover's arms
Wants flow as the sea
In your lover's arms
Hunger soothed by the feed
The limits are none
And I'll show you my weakness
As you burn in my strength
As I am strong

Wandered and hopeful
Near and undressed
Falling in miracles
Fortunes are besting us

Awake and undaunted
As sure as we flow
As sure as we know
The endless need

In the space of your heart
Storms met by their end
In the space I know my friend
The lover's friend.

Feeling

Don't mistake me for a stranger
It's been too cold this winter
And I know I'm not alone
In this feeling
It's got me feeling for you

Don't mistake me for a stranger
It could be ten thousand years
And I know it would be the same
In this feeling
The way it's breathing in you

Do you see my reach out?
Do you feel the motion for you?
Do you want my reach out?
Do you mind the falling for you?

No one has ever felt this way
No one has ever caused this race
No other feels the way you do
And you keep on pulsing
You keep on pulsing in me
But I never get tired
And I never get tired from you
So come on love, come down to me

Don't mistake me for a stranger
I know you've tasted cold winters
But know that I am home for you
In this feeling
In this sealing to you

Do you love my reach out?
I love your reach out
I love when you reach out for me
In this feeling
In this feeling.

As Spoken

The mind is imagination
But the heart is all of truth
And when I feel, and when I see
The reality finds me buried
I wandered too long in dancing
I shipped blank letters out to sea
Ate the feast of mankind cravings
But love did not scold me
It saturated my famine
Gave meat to my ailing mass
Reminded me the life of my being
Gave rebirth when death called me
It sheltered the heat from burns
Cleared the scars fought in hard
Sexed my body and soul completely
For love, with its unfailing hold
Enfolded my every reason.

Thief

It was not before I could go
Walk into his skin
And sin the dear out of his restraint
No budge, no try, he said
No sin upon my saint
But little did he know
We are one the same
Equal names and frames
To merge unearthly, and it hurt
Yet for now, wishes to wind to say
You will always be
The thief of my laced soul.

Will

Mazing through mind fields
The water swims me deep
Gazing through crystal eyes
The thick requests my sleep
I want to rest again
To rest a first time
But God, does the quickening come?

Awake for years
Asleep for daydreams
I come, I come, succumb

Whitening the winter
Painting for the spring
Past of years, a gone for good
The heart knows what it means
To touch again
To touch a first time
Let unearthly passion reign

Apart for years
So close in daydreams
Do come, do come, succumb

For it was you and it was I
Here ever still
It wills, it's us
It calls our name and still refrains
Forever the same
It wills us two
To one, to one, in love.

Release

Upon a press of heart
I go weak
Escapable I'm not
To this expose
I love the way it hurts
When it's going to ease the burn
In my fall, in me falls
To my own high

Hard to catch a thief
Let them go
Keep the love not the pain
Make the calm in arms
I love the way it hurts
The last to be the first
I be all, I be all
To my own hands

And bless the rain
Soaking in the skin
Lifting hands above
The full becomes enough
And the hauntings roam away
So far away

I press my heart
And find there's breath
Sinking in the thick of it
And letting go
No more walls, no more walls
To my own love.

Saturation

In your desert where it's barren
Have you tasted saturation from my flow?
For this water is the ocean
You are captain, tame the beast
Have I awoken your sleeping beauty?
Do your eyes look out to see?

One

I am of one, a dove
A flight of wings, I soar
I sleep the ground, a friend
Nature is my beast

I am of one, a son
A child of light, I grow
I learn in time, a path
Nature is my beast

I am of one, a crust
A heart of Earth, I pulse
I feel all wounds, a graze
Nature is my beast

I am of one, a love
A gift of truth, I live
I am for all, a need
Nature is my beast

A beast of beauty
A beauty of light
But all in time
And out of my mind.

End of War

Its been met
If you finish dying then you're dead
But here I stand breathing again
Spreading love like wildfire

And those who quivered
Will know comfort shivers
In my spanned embrace
They will know forgiveness
In caress and undress from my eyes
A million miles, a million weights
Shall release a million waves
Of ecstacy

Alarms you had
Alarms that drove you mad
Explode as I do
They never sang you truth
For in your arms
The angel of my goddess
My woman to your man
Yes, blood was lost
And caused such misery
But lover, it was fleeting

The Heavens rained, stars collided
Bursting scenes for us to find
A sigh of glory hallelujah
So exhale the breath you're holding in
Release the tension
And sink in godsend
Like it's all you've ever known
God knows we've reached the end of war
So let me carry you
Through the door of love unfailing

Yes, its been said
If you finish dying
Then you're dead
So take my hand this very night
For we shall live again.

Veil Falls

Take me to thy chamber
Tie me to thy sex
Out the hands, out the lips
The veil falls down
The win of love exists

The convenience of a safety
We barricade a storm
And so it will rise
And so it will rage on mighty voice
But to it I make an equal wall of taste

As it was demons set out to destroy
Yet so close to death
An end of feverish wisps
By the whispers of almighty prayers

In ties with heavened convoys
Fire to fire come nigh
Cast off the burning liege
It was a siege of none
A captive of none, never be

Into the dark returned
Shadows to feed off the gold
Standing in waste and fatigue
Saw I you savoring me
Reviving my heart
As no one never knew through

As you are here and we are real
Ingest every dynastic brace
With breath, without
Leave bodies no room
Now creators, left to their need

For once a seed seemed so vast
And as endless time
It was grown past all adore
And resets in its glow and after
Bare to bare in capture.

Facing

In rainstorms, standing
Wet until my bones feel damp
I'm tasting the bite of my lip
Then close my eyes and count to ten
When I open them
Be facing me, laughing
Crying, ready for ecstasy
Glowing the dark and encompassing light
The fire and ice of the living tree.

Kundalini

Beseech the sun because I insist
To see the sky burn flames
Of my name in deep engrave
Written by love's pale hand

Summon the moon because I infuse
The light, the dark to be one
With vapors, my mist compelling
Spelling the wake from my dreams

And in line my spine of force
The power to ooze out of me
In veins flow, in heart beat mast
In body envelop the beast

And from the ground rise forth
Slither around all my limbs
Then in karma eat my spine
And activate my life.

Fire

The hottest tongue
To the loudest fire
Stir the burn with words
As if the skin would melt and crawl
Away from all your bones
I cannot recall
Ever knowing I flamed you
But just a hint of a spark
Behind a hidden heart barely beating
Was the phantasmal reach
Into my very life

Said the weaker frame
To the proudest stand
Turn and walk into the sun
As if the earth would come to die
A thousands deaths
Away from being alive
I cannot recall
Ever knowing I moved you
But there more further beyond
The bridge weighing me about to fall
Was an enslaving glance
Into my very eyes

And at the last break and the air hit
I closed my eyes and wrapped my arms
Around my body tight
As further flew I spread my wings
Like a bird and fell to the earth
Burned and moved
Beyond myself
A melt into the ground

But as time passes on
The weak becomes strong
And what's eternity
Will always burn deep
So if I flamed you, if I moved you
Did you not know you did me too?

Temple

Mercy to my foe
Who stirs inside of me
Wearing my body
Like a dress for upscale insist
When feeling so heavy
Sinking into my bed
I repeat words I've said to do me well
Words I've said to loose the chain
Regaining my wits again
To pull my temple up from waste
And walk right out the door

There is sun, it seems
Inching into this room
Like searching for me
A creep to soothe and light once more
I bore so much
Now purge it out to be
Burned into something grand in azure
I repeat words I've said to find breath
Words I've said to clear the head
Bending but never to break
To pull my temple up from pain
And run right out the door

I wore this first
This mass of skin
And to hand it off the greater sin
Because I want to feel unbound
To laugh to cry to love to die
So foe, before you go
Raise you glass and drink it slow
Ingest your strain and see me weightless
You poisoned your own sly

I repeat words I've said with no tongue
Words I've said to kiss goodbye
Inspiring heart to beat and feet to move
And pull my temple up again
To dance right out the door.

Creeping Dawn

As if I'll never be the same
I relapse to an old form
Of standing drenched in rain
Never knowing the difference
Until I've caught fever again

The chill is the dream
Without it, I'm on edge
Of silence sold estranged
Walking through invisible seduces of air
And bare feet burning from Earth heat
Hypnotized by the creeping dawn

Of time a daft reminder
It's now to rise once more
But I ask aloud
What if I choose sleep?
To keep from losing love
The spinning fancies me
God, won't it tire?
When I long to bathe in pools
Of ecstasy, both body and spirit

If its words, then hear it
But watch how my eyes shift haze
Reflecting the frail fragility
Decorated for decoding
This rain in breaking kind

As if I'll never by the same
As if I'll never be immortal
As if I'll never wake again.

Die Me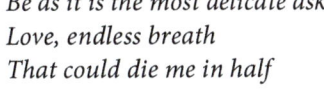

Forbid the glow escaping this moon
It's tired and restless
In sleep all too soon
Long such the night, of which we came
Embracing mind's vision
Of lovers ingrained

Bring forth the time
I was free in true quiet
Soul pushing open the door to my riot
Flowing in blood to spirit in essence
One face like mine
Comes again each candescent

Be as it is the most delicate ask
Love, endless breath
That could die me in half

Such person revealed, a true ever known
Over wandered, wild mercy is shown
Life upon life, beat after beat after beat
Distance so sour, the hunger so sweet

Grounded, I'm heavy, deep in hard grief
It's bloody, violent and screaming relief
Both of us dead and buried before
Resurrection comes still to silence the war

Be as it is the most delicate ask
Love, endless love
That could die me in half

My vessel covers an earth's piece of skin
I speak with the Heaven's
With no move of lips
Aligned are we beings, pulled to our save
Step follow step leads yours to my face

Risen our highers are guiding recover
Love of the soul and love of each other
For every night, and for every light
Shared of the two are life and soul sighs

Be as it is the most delicate ask
Love, endless breath
That could die me in half

Be as it is, as it is
Be as it is, as it is
Be as it is, this most delicate ask.

Fragile

Fragile me
At loss for words
The silence I am in
Who sees me
Not following
With nothing to let on

To ever be exposed
I am what no one knows
You come too close
You come too close

For fragile you
At loss in translation
The love you bear in hold
Come for me
Is there ravishing?
This heaven we be in

To ever be exposed
The parts I've always froze
You come so close
You come so close

Yet every sense exudes
The need to be with you
I have no fight
By pools divine
Hear these shivers
And down your descent
I will not fight.

Enemy

Time is the enemy
Patience, its weapon of choice
The choke it leaves me
Unable to breathe

Voices in the night
Dancing on the desert wind
Call me to the night
To follow them

I long to be near you
I long to be near you

My safety cried defense
Formed as walls of solid fear
To mask the weakness
Of my mind confused
And the loneliness of the aged heart
Struggles to suppress
Chances of true happiness

I long to be with you
Yet I cannot be near you
I cannot be near you now

Then a trembling hand reaches out
The depth has become my end
So I will climb, I will climb
As high as love will allow
And if there is strength
And the beat of unconditional love
The enemy will not prevail
Not prevail over me

I will be with you
Yes, I will be with you

Oh, time
Time was the enemy
But an enemy unprevailing
Never to prevail over me.

Burn

For every day I've known you
And for every day forever
A million prayers assemble
Ascend to the Heavens and shake

For every kiss to touch my lips
And for every one to follow
A thousand emotions take control
Fueling the fire within

You bring joy, you bring pain

Burn into my soul, my soul
Burn deep into my soul

For every soulful tear I've shed
And for every one to come
A hundred shivers blanket me
Freezing each moment I hold

For every ache felt locked inside
And for every ache to release
Only one heart longs for you
Offering endless love

You bring joy, you bring pain

Burn into my soul, my soul
Burn deep into my soul

Be careful, be reckless
Burn into my soul
Stay focused, stay always
Burn deep into my soul

For every day forever
A million prayers assemble
Ascend into the Heavens

For you are my joy
You are my pain.

Sparrow

Sparrow, fly
High from me now
Vacant is my sleep
Give taste of wind
On feathered skin
Grace my soul to keep

Still over mountains
Still through valleys
Journey to the parts of me
I still hold remiss
May hope engulf my soul

Sparrow, cry
Loud for me now
Silence was my mouth
Lost voice in truth
As for me to constitute
Every reason to be found

Still pass roses wilting
Still above terrain
Journey to the parts of me
Too long contained
May hope engulf my soul
May hope diminish the reign of ache
May hope know only love

So arrow to my heart
And aim my sparrow deep
Then sparrow, my sparrow
Rise high within me now.

Melt

Tangle, the season is over
She's ready to melt in the sun
She's me in the best way unveiled
And if you're as wise as we think
Never take like a thief

But give like a lover
As a nurturing mother
And share as you would
Dare to be naked and free
I see you, so see me

Live in our town
And live in our country
Hunt me and want me
For life, all in life

In case of miles to pour over
I'm ready, as you're feeling strong
Faster and faster come
Work with what gets the feat done
To make it with your lady fair

And you're like no other
As I'm under and over speaking
Let's hear what you think
In need to be open and free
I see you, you see me

Live in our town
And live in our country
Hunt you and want you
For life, all in life
So hunted and wanted
For life, all our life
In our tangle of melts in the sun.

Will Fall

If any one dares to see
I will not show me weak
I cannot let them in
Only lead a cool front
Hold up a wrecking ball
Saving it for love and more
I'll be alone in myself
Until it is right, and then I will fall
Watch me as I will fall
Catch me when I will fall

Faces walk by without care
I know it in each empty stare
Tell me how long will it be
Until I see you and you dare me
Looking up to weathered skies
Wanting to live from your eyes
I've always relied on myself
But I cannot deny I have fallen
Watch me as I am fallen
Catch me when I am fallen

Tell me why all defenses erase
And I am fine, every part of me safe
And I'm all and I'm in
And I know this is it, I'm in love

To be vulnerable at its convey
Some deep and delicate taste
Hold on, I'm burning within
The turning around of this life
For I have fallen
Watch me as I have fallen
Catch me as I have fallen
Hold me, I've fallen with you.

Jump

Guarded up my fever
Kept a straight face in the light
You told me nothing
Yet showed me everything

Boarded up every window
No glancing in without say
We've lost all these things
But what lies lingering
Is only for a day

All the grieves ate through me
No living for the rain
All the thieves called your fingers
Sometime I pray will find their graves

It will make the difference to you
Because you let it run
Jump on the train
Speed away, speed away

It will not hold resistance from me
As you see me leave
Jump on the train
Speed away, speed away

Jump on the train
Speed away.

Speech of Seas

Once petrified, I sank
Down in mounds of ache
And drank from prison cups
Poison to my love
Destitute from sorrow
Would not beg, steal nor borrow
For the weight I was in
Was the thick of my create
Yet I reached

The frailing of my hands
Continued out from me
For you see, hope is not a thrill
And will never be killed
Though it may bleed
Though it may pour
Rivers from sores and pulls
When called a tender fool
The day of dawn, its love comes full

So from ground I rise
I fight to look you in the eyes
And speak the seas of care
Being fully naked, fully bare
Regardless of return
And should it be
The touch is the same
I will let this flame burn
My honour to be graced
And know the face of you evermore

This love I give, I gave to me
In the bury of my deep
So is my deserve
Is this love heard?
Is this love known?
Is this love owned?
And shared by one who sees
The beauty that is me
Strong and weak.

I n W eep

The crashing sea pleads
Come bathe in me
But alas, my fall on sand
Landed on back
Under sky forming kisses
Heavens appearing so endless
Could I be timeless?
When a world burns around
When death and pain ring in ears

How sweet the wind be
Moving over naked skin
Making shivers like fevers
I've been under the cover of ache
Suffocating…
I hated to be without and longing
But it was wrong to spend so long
In midnights while in daylights
So say, God, I rage for release

Driving rains
Pouring as a thundering king
Fears escape
Causing my massive tremble
As the earth cradles me
A love making eyes bleed tears
Pushes the spear out of me
Could this be dying?
Take my body, and my spirit

Senses numbing
Then shattering glass, they lash
Apart the poison
So emotions explode and speed
As rivers beast into the sea
Inhaling breath unknown
Throw me away so my truth will stay

And motion me on into eternity
So I may be in weep of heaves
When I weep the sea.

Ship & Sea

My world flows around me
Then through me in diamond shine
And the crystals held with eyelids
Radiate an ocean in siege

There's a captain, he stands afar
Ready, yet unsure of how
For his ship is his only love
He cannot bear her threat in storms

As she watches his watch over
Comes the stone of his protect
But in her goddess sees his weaving
Of beauty known to her and God

Her eyes weeping from the storm clouds
He denied to have her wave
Reaching, seeking through the thick fog
The soul will find her equaled mate

She will remind him he's the captain
Meant to hand and man his ship
Burning raindrops lead frail mist
Lead to dark clouds broken by sun

Then she peers him on calm horizon
He meets her stare and reaches out
Yes, my world flows around me
Then through me in diamond shine

And this captain entwined with me
Savors the throw of ship and sea.

Ghost, Hunter

Into a summer rain
Like a wind pushes direction
I face the way I burn and run to you
Let the sky explode
And sound rattle the soul
For I know now
What it is you asked of me
And I know now
What it is I truly need
Of desire, a fire
Long sacred in my heart
Of passion, action
Long awaited to be freed

What will you do with me?
I stand before you
At helm a lovers reign
And patent to soak the taste
See if eternal lasts
The blissful kiss
The hardened touch
The merging stare
So bare it all
Then when we fall
Be no more a watchful ghost

Be the skin
That warms me thick
And the hunter of these lands
Where a summer rain
This summer rain
Swallows less the liquid you
Don't move, let me see
The fear deceased and us at peace
Finding love after the storm.

Guardian

Tempers few
She wishes not to burn
But the heart flushes
The blood fuels
The fumes come
For one loved
Has hurt from devils

She can reign from fire
When aimed to save
The evidence against hell
Serves her well to stand
Hand to heart
The other apart to air
The shield so
Thrown like a spear
On target

She can silence fear
When aimed to brave
The protest declining hell
Serves her tell expelling
Hand to heart
The other apart to air
The force so
Flown through as an arrow
To the target

Lepers of demons
Legions move to pull
Down the love
But last not so
For the bow
From arrow
Slices all.

Immersed

There she stands
Near yet so afar
Her eyes in impassioned gleam
She is unveiling

And she could just be
Completely immersed
By the hands of melody
Crawling in her veins
Breathing her wake

Let me be in this, dear God
Let me be in this

And she could just be
Completely immersed
Taken in her lover's body
Racing through his veins
Breathing his taste

Let me be in this, dear God
Let me be in this

And she would sleep
Inside a blissful kiss
And she would wake
Intake a breathless crest

And she loves
And as she loves
Completely immersed
So she soars

Let me be in this, dear God
Let me be all of this.

Taste

I can forget you
If the world burns in fire
And every scream outlasts the pain

I can forget love
When the winter freezes me
And my body breaks
In pieces unmatched

I had to tell you this
I was poisoned by your kiss
In this blaze of memory
Nothing is concrete

How could you leave
With so much love
How could you block
And lock me in you

But I can forget hope
In letters of words once written
And every latitude proves it was vain

I can forget us
Should my mind fate escape
And thieves succeed
In claiming victory

You should have told me
Fear was destined over love
For laughter fades from river tears
Fast flowing without fail

I let you leave
No christened goodbye
No last lovemaking
So cruelly dazed
I'll never fall again
You'll have to live alone

Sexed by regret, unable to forget
As only I, I tried
Opened by the fire
Let the soaring flame brave
In a taste I'd never known
If without you

But I can forget you
I can.

Boil

I've been maddened
Wondering if I'm alive
And if the flare caught in my person
Was in truth or mortal lie

I've been suckled in such fever
My body's never known
All because hope won't die
And fights to overthrow

The way it seeps, I'm at your will
Indisposed and no one knows
How I've come and now become
Something in a form of love

And darling, it's daring me
Declaring who I've always been
The thinking mind, by sheer entice
Is boil rising it out of me

Like shimmering gold at throw
Away from my fair skin
So thick and powerful
I did not know could stab within

If words could ever mate
The way your essences saturated
It would be all that I could do
To live what we create

I've been maddened, I've been suckled
And the proof is me on knees
Gasping for breath, tears flowing
Until a heart resets it's beat.

Daylight

In a moment, none became the same
Engulfed by flaming highs
A desperate fear to run and hide
Oh, dying by a pressure wound
No one could heal nor could consume
An endless hour on bended knees
Rioting darkness inside of me

For countless came the yearning sleep
The draw from you, the give to be
As lying on our sides, I would embed
The feeling of fervor
The gods once had said
Will open a vessel and set forth the sail
To define all heaven and quiet all hell

Yet in the daylight
Oh, in spite of love
He took away

By far remained in a drowning lake
Swallowed in pull and letting it take
To know what's well and still be declined
Is a damning sickness you plead to survive
Such penetrating cold to seep every bone
To question the feel
And question the home

Though years at pass
So stings the weakened creep
The scent of you, the promise to be
Lying on our backs, you will embed
The feeling of fervor
The gods once had said
Will open a vessel and set forth the sail
To define all heaven and quiet all hell

Yet in the daylight and night
Oh, in spite of love
He holds away

Oh how does thou wound
As much as thou cares
You taint all my reach out
So alone in my bare
I've prayed for our silence
So that I may live
And love to another
Who will give as I give

You weave and you wrestle
Make fool with love
Do they know you live me
When touched in your lust?
Oh, how does thou lie
As much as thou feels me?

To bide in a winter of infinite course
Would bury the light
In the weight of remorse
After my sleep, then shall I rise
I'll do as my heart to never think twice
If with is without you, I move to release
For freedom is bliss
Not distance the beast

And in the daylight
Oh, in spite of love
I may breathe
And breathe another lung

Oh, you may choose
In love what you do
But need you know
As I grow, I will grow
And when I do
Be you not my equal
I must bid, I must kiss
You adieu
In the daylight.

Dark Cupid

And so it was a crow
For better and for worse
Neglecting the world to privy me
And against the western wind
The feathers expand in brim
Forecast the raging storm in tow

The beauty of his folly
Was envisioned arrow and bow
Like a cupid but dark in darkened dress
And the power of his stress
Forced me look into his eye
Be not afraid, he spoke
It is time for you to die
And rise again the honey dawn

For walls around your heart are strong
But stronger is your love
And to the man who ingests you
The one in vulnerability to be
He surrounds as you burn circles

Out the flame, now take his hand
Know the bare of more than skin
Know the give of raging heaves
Know the beauty that he sees
For it is you and you conceive
The majestic regal blood
Regal bones and come and blush
From your eyes see more than view
Your time is now and love is due.

The Weeping

Red, her eyes after crying
Gold, when shone in the light
Navy, at the stir of her lover
But lost at death of her love

Tragic and grief
Raging swords dove
Deep into her back
So much blood

Darkness even in day
Earth rose as she collapsed
Ground, sound of silence thick
Yet deafening the wide

Every mountain emotion
Unearthly yet it kept
The violence of a shiver
When again the widow wept

Wept for every touch
Knew in the rush of blood
Knew in the gentle need
Of intimate reach

Wept for every kiss
Knew in the press of lips
Knew in the gentle brush
Of lifelong blush

For her passion
For her equality
For her gratitude
And all his love.

Lay the Fullness

Words drowned as tears fell
How he ached to confess everything
For too long pass
Yet how the seasons of life
Sweep through a clear kaleidoscope

When faith and belief had died
Hope still slept with her
Pulling her upwards
From the depth of a pool of red
A mind asunder, a heartbeat pained
At every next flow

If only to know honest
Did such a creature exist?
Yes, but more than her wish
As the hands of this man
Tremble at the flesh of her face
To escape in her eyes
He longed to many times
Yet demons at play and at sly
Weathered every favor
Scattered every plan

But in the end
He and she have landed
In a world, in a field
On a blanket, fully naked
And forgiving the gulfs of delay

And the dearest part is
That man did say
What he needed to say
All in the strength of a kiss
In which lay the fullness to bathe
In love for a lifetime beyond.

Armies Up

The mirror of white reflects my chill
Over hills and mountains I can't climb
All to find the glory of a hero
High or low, the true is what we dare

In the darkness I begin
To grow the light I died within
The enemy of my own wounded heart
In the tempting of the cold
I voice words I've never told
The silence of my own wounded guard

Armies up and aimed to face winter's seep
All to free and victor I can't view
The dawning hues take wrap of my skin
Thick or thin the truth of what we bare

From the darkness I unwind
To grow the light I feared to find
The enemy of my own wounded heart
In the tempting of the hold
I voice words I've yet to bold
The silence of my own wounded guard

It's hard and it's dreadful
All the beautiful blood was spilt
But I will rise and reign, mighty
Come storms in rage or pain.

With the darkness I attain
To grow the light I had to become
The enemy of my own wounded heart
In the tempting of the wait
I voice words I've had to brave
The silence of my own wounded guard

Wounded hard
But come so far
Far to speak the truth.

Wastelands

As hearts in heavy
They weigh and they pull
When my heart bears heavy
The dam bursts in full
The earth burns in fire
The sun dresses to night
Heaven readies her soldiers
For a convalescent fight

Such battlefields beholding
Never a leveled pass
Who knew without my indulging
This temperament to last
The pressure reaches limits
The ache so soon explodes
Existence breaches all corners
For a luminescent show

Battlefields, battlefields
Wastelands they become
Choke the smoke and view the damage
Wake me if I've won
I leave this skin and rise above
The picture stretches wide
So much involved, too much was lost
The karmic great divide

What words to say I've seen, I've heard
The journey mustn't cease
Pray God for strength to rise again
And travel the road to peace

So bearer be light and shoot with zeal
Aim to the very core
Exhaust all beat of fear regretted
Anchor ships onto the shore
As the sky enters gold vapors
The night reveals the day
Finding life within my willing breath
In all incandescent ways.

Parting

How cryptic the words spoke
As if there had been choking
Rolling in my bed
Until we found a breath
It was a lovely parting
Then days of famine, so estranged
I'll never be fooled again
That's what I said because I did

Upon a month it was
Came attempt to call my name
You damn bastard
Melt sinfully into your shame
I wish me well and time can tell
I'm truly meant for love
So enjoy your lust
I'll never trust but only myself from you

Who are you? It matters not
Just a lesson caught and learned
And the burn I feel in my chest
Is the love to steal my heart
A heart, I hope you find yours
Buried firm in gross disguise
But your gossamer eyes show it through
The cold will fever you

While I live in open truth
Finding love to your alone
Don't worry dear, the cut will heal
Just not the creep into your bones
And for that
You're welcome.

Savory

While away the winter grew
Cold beyond an ice
The blood drew thin
As masking of my sin begat a smile
As though my hide away
Was some beguiling of a man
Free to roam and nothings loan
As I if I never was

But oh, how he cries now
The dying of our love
Oh, how he dies now
For he once thought it too much
Kind but all too sweet
Tempting but all too gentle

Few hours spent in throws of skin
He melted from assuming pins
One's that prick the skin
And drain the blood
Yet no touch mine
The fool, the mighty fool
Come seeking lovers base
But so estranged

As now he longs to love in right
And in this time grew fragile nights
The dimming of her light had tasted dark

And a heart fell apart
Heavied as it shed
Oceans deep and heaving
From her breast

She stares through
Yet can you see her soul?
Can you prove to her
Without her you're unwhole?
Is because of her there is no other
For she needs no father, no brother
But a lover
Equal to the force beyond compare

Can you wear her ins and outs?
Her soul and her body
Not the way you doubt
Owning of your truth and all be still
Move mountains in your reach of her
Through hell and more so sure endure
For the merging of your beasts
And angels twined

Time is melting fast young lad
Savory is best, but be it your test
Your moves, your decide
To win or lose, bear your truth
Oh God, grant the light of dawn to love.

Think

Come away with something waking
Come away with something saying
You will never be the same
Stay away until it eats you
Stay away until you need this

Listen to the words I'm saying
Listen to the heart inside you racing
You will never be the same
Come around when you have loved us
Come around when you want for this

Thinking of your reposition
Is all you can afford to see
Thinking of your cinematic entrance
To a steep and fast decline

You are eager to hold on
Yet barely in a fused embrace
Why don't you try falling of love
Why don't you get lost inside it now
The way you long be

Not afraid to love you madly
Not afraid to want you so bad
Think it over, think about it
In the end it's how you feel.

Imagine Shadows

When I sleep
What furthers your intrigue
As you sing my demise?
Suppose the darkness
Hid me from your view
It would be the one thing
I would long of you
Because I'm tried

You write upon
The meekness of my heart
What distances your body to my rise
Imagine shadows kiss me, unlike you
It could erase the hold I've dared undo
Because it's time

No amount of suffering
Changes where I'm weakened
The petty things of your pretty things
Have only faded my cool flame
Now it's late, and I'm so tired

I hold no anger to your lack of mercy
For I tied unconditional
Between the air we breathe
It shall not break, for my behalf
But do not believe
My love inside can't hold me up

How has your face
Imprinted behind my eyes
What kind of elegance
Plays upon my mind

Pretend moonlights
Show amounts of truth
It's me and dying
To wrestle from wounds
Because we're hurt

You surface from the truth
You have of me
What part of love diseased
What beauty called?
Assume heart stops give way your fool
It's breaking down walls
And all too soon
Because you need me

No amount of coldness changed
Where you're not as strong
The petty stings of our pretty strings
Have only lost some precious times
It's late, and now you're tired

Release the fear to lack of belief
For we're ties unconditional
Between the air we breathe
It shall not cease, for my behalf
But do not think
Your love inside has me to lose
Oh, it's late, so late we're tired

I'm reminded tomorrow is soon
Let's quiet fevers and silence love aches
And pray, pray true
We can be renewed.

Heroes

The tears have passed, my lover
For given the need of your heart
Cross not the night up in arms
When in favor and savor of care
Express forth the turnings in mind
Every detail as deep to explore
Breathe fire, the natural explode
Hold nothing back in love attacks

Make love as never beguiled you
An erupting volcano to appease
Unraveling the strings of carnation
Uniting as leaders of love in war
Make love as never became you
A devilish mistress in peace
Unleashing reverence to erotic
Uniting as heroes of love in war.

Daze

To live a body, man holds breath
And beat, I feel when touching chests
Eyes to eyes, the daze comes in
Yet grounded by the heated skin
The share of secret, we bold us free
Complete into you, complete into me.

Blush

I'm in blush
I want to sin
To grasp the tip
Of everything firing me
As a volcano needs the air
With fare of heat
Mouth of yours
Exhaust into me
Smiles both free and bare
Within arms of landing
Barrowing deep we aim

Love be the name and ecstacy the veins
Wrapped around every inch and pinch
Till the scream sings as the eyes faint
When the moments pause to affect

Each whole exhumed
With no reach past
Only clutch for clutch
From none of lust
We long as long we do

In the dark of the day, victories
The stare hungers never to be pulled
The need to stay weds into the light
Does not leave, does not rest as we do

Laying entered
Still bonded tight
As if the long known dream
Becomes as we've come on
Rolled into one
The intricate sum
Each touch it burns
And sweets the tongue
We cannot, shall not get enough
With no wonder, nor no wander
I'll live as you love as you live as I love
So long as long we do.

Heart

Carus, carus
I'm inward too bound
Straining from captive
And gasping for breath
Feeling burdened, fatigued
But braving to exile
I pray, enim diligo

Carus, carus
Much time in these lengths
Wading from fallacy
With a grip on my pure
Wasted in wastelands
And calling to transcend
I pray, enim diligo

The swaddle in obey
The truth never conveyed
Said not to be the exception
Follow or taste that of hell

Carus, carus
Weaken this cocoon
Mercy thy handle
To expel such unholy
Believe I'm believed
And pressing awakened
I pray, enim diligo

Carus, carus
I'm sensing the moment
Rapidly in high degree
Reverence per my request
For savoring strength
But owning my beauty
I pray, enim diligo

The swaddle falls away
The truth reaches release
Say now I'm the exception
To embrace in eternus flamma.

At A Loss

This undying fire
And I dream still of you
Visions unfold
All we need is the truth
What wraps around this pulse
Keeps at haze in the mist
The hands seem empty
But the body is filled

Daylight lies down
And I'm loosing the fear
When I won't give in
There's hope in deaf ears
The movement of time
Is speeding for want
The hands find entwine
And in circle they run

Wake me
I chose to wake from the dark
The dark died the depth of me
Of which I thought loss
Now the essence is changing
And charging with seed
And we cry at the come
Of a living dream.

Close

If ever all you wanted came to be
Would you grasp, would you release?
If ever all you wanted was me
Would you be happy?

If ever all you wanted loved the most
Would you fear, would you be bold?
If ever all you wanted was me
Would you feel lucky?

Fools to run, we take so long
Fools to fight but we hold on
Apart for nothing
Close, don't come

If ever all you wanted wants you too
If ever all you wanted wants you too
What do you choose?
Win or lose, sink or swim, live or die
Would you try?

If ever all you wanted moved away
Would you pass, would you make haste?
If ever all you wanted was me
Would you speak need?

Fools to lie in others arms
Fools to brave such still guards
Apart for nothing, apart for nothing
Close, don't come

We never come, too close
We strain the hope and die the rose
It fails to show
The love we hold away

If ever all you wanted parted life
Would you sigh, would you too die?
If ever all you wanted was me
Would you still breathe?

Oh, Love, my fool
What say you do?
If it was I you had
Would it be so bad to be with me?

Pull

As I see
You hide with dark and light
As you see
I'm yours until I'm right
Because you're mine, you say
Because I'm not, I say
Don't fight the pull in full
I cannot stay

As you want
Every inch of soul bodied
As I want
To taste and be set free
Because you're mine
Outside of time, you say
Because I'm not
A lover caught, I say
Don't fight the pull in full
I cannot stay

We cannot stay this way
We cannot be that way

Don't go
Don't let go, you say
Let me go, I pray
Away, so far away

I must go and as I go
Hear this final, friend
This time is my end
This time is the end.

Air

Filled with too much
Such a tender reeve
To move the lover's air

You don't weave us easy
Like we'd want to show
Words my gentle weapon
Don't go

Matched for wit and thought
Caught up in spotlight
Here but still lost somewhere
To find the lover's air

You don't dress this easy
Like we'd want to show
Words fall in hard undress
Please, don't go

Somewhere in the smoke
Comes the lover
Somewhere moving in
Comes the lover
Inhaling, breath within
The lover's air daring me

Oh you've kept me waiting
I've paid my last respects
Every part undone and alone
To merging shadows on the wall

Calling out to you
Don't go again
Take a second thought
Don't go again, don't go
Please don't go.

Proud Sea

Closer
I can fall
In simple yearning
In the night
I can see
The candle dying

Bolder than I
You can be
In blissful hiding
In the dark
You can feel
The whispers starting

Match the steps
You can find
They await matching
As we make
Embrace of arms
There go the charms of time

Closer to me
In the night
I can see
Your ageless beauty
As you take
My breath away

Where roses birth
Where shadows rest
The tender wind blows
When minutes pass
When lovers sigh
The gentle wave crashes
The mass of the proud sea.

Harvest

If but a winter
May be I'll turn
Do I wait with bated breath
Beyond the reason of love?
All for a promise
Stay, then I'll leave
Do I wish in cold counterfeit
Beyond the reason of love?

When I felt the glass before it broke
Desire overwhelmed the fear it invoked
The slits of my hands coloured in red
And down came the body to harvest the bed

As still a lover fevering my veins
Near or far, weak or strong
I'd die this way again
Only for you.

Maze

It's hard to have hope when you're haunted
A maze that continually changes
The hollowed out beast
Breathes the air robbed of me
Can I, can I let go?
God, mercy strength where devils roam
Is this a winter that freezes my soul
For shall I go?

And I can never reprieve
There's no reason ever be
Shown to the depths of despair
Hell has no room for me there
So Heaven, be to me kind
Give light in the dark and enflame my heart
As I lay, as I lay me down.

Musk Traces

Like a lady
But restless to sin
On levels few men seek
He looked of grim
I knew it
But not why
Only gave my eyes to him

On a Tuesday
Month of spring release
Heavy in my mind
Into my skin he tapped
Bared us both in glance
We knew it
Overpowered and afraid

As if days had passed in seconds
Flowers grown and died
I could say ten in years
Some vision
Might have been
Or not be
Cannot guess my heart

Like thief
Gone with no shame
Let the hope flee
I'd rather have me true
In no belief
Questions rose
When I met the cold

Only lingers of musk
Slight traces of no shave
Crawl into bed with me
If I could fill my dreams
They would be red
Ribbons strung of gold
And dancing
So much dancing
With toes upon the snow.

Dagger

In night I have come
Resolute to my fix
You air a dangerous quiver
Be it wrong then I die
For once to lay bare
In the tresses of urgency

I'm wicked in thought
But need is a grave
The idea we are free
Yet a slave to your slave
In silence, I am
In cold silence

Acts the sting to my will
No quarrel could I sound
When wisdom is beyond our years
From tears to a smile
Take a while to attend
Send misery to hell's adore

The weapon on your person
Marked me as the hunted
Plunge the dagger down into my core
Make me sore in repent
In screams as I sweat
Sire, free bare me full

Only tiresome from ache
But not the bold of permeate
It was my deed, within our test
If one survives, I'll go to rest
In meadows of my very soul

You know it was right, just as I
We are tied to the kindles of time
As a fire to never know end
Time before
Time of now
And once again.

Dragon

Fallen in, fallen fast
Night closed in and came the chance
Something called and pulled us close
Dark lips as the satin rose
And it said, kiss the dragon

Met you once, remember me
Fortune and fame felt it yet to be
Patience waling, looking on
Words of hope created the song
And it sings, kiss the dragon

Rain to taste, rain I feel
Lonely times begin to heal
Something found in those eyes of blue
Returned again only for you
And we said, kiss the dragon
And we kiss, kiss the dragon.

Let Me

Let me in. I'm getting tired
For one night, don't quiet the fire
When I burn loud with you
As you sleep, I'm lying beside
For this night, our dreams run wild
See me dream loud with you

Take my hand I'm reaching out
You and I in love flowing fast
When from the touch need takes hold
What you feel is your return
No surprise the way we react
See the dawn come on too fast

It's so easy and only so right
Let me in, let me see
This is the night.

 We Are

All the hope that's left between us
Shooting down another flame
You can shoot an arrow at a tame heart
And never see a drop of blood
Walk a thousand miles in a dark night
Bare to the pain all because

You never knew
You thought you could
You left the lot to me
To hold onto

You can tear the heart a million times
Level ground with a single glance
Cross the desert on bare, scarred feet
All to say you could be mine
Hands apart are reaching out now
Find the skin and crawl inside

You had to see
We couldn't be without
You kept a lot deep down
To come on strong to me this way

There could be a different ending
When all the lights are going down
Lift the body, match a heartbeat then
Let the wanting be found again
You had to see, you had to see

Every lover knows the hardship
Of holding on when all alone
Every heart resets its beating
When the wandered ship
Comes sailing home

You had to be
How you've always been
You had to let me know
You're always the one.

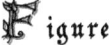 Figure

If alone
I am thundered
And hungered for you
If opened
I am reaching
And breaching for you

When night closes in
You speak as the wind
In the inside
And I forget time
You walk in my mind
As the weaver

And there's still your figure
Drawn beside my whisper
Oh, there's yet a wedded
To be bedded in love
Calling for you

In absence
Rages moments
Gone missing from you
In full respect
Comes all to give
What's been hid from you

Then love humbles in
You show us the things
We've been needing
And I go insane
In how you say my name
As the weaver
And the feeder of truth

Fallen for you like no other
There's no other
Just each other
In the middle of existence
Fallen through truth.

Lip & Tongue

You're in thick
I'm wearing thin of hope
And allowing the day
To stroke the curves of my heart
I could wander for days
Spend hours in the dunes
The corners that hold in the mind

But I'm over it and it's overdue
I step into the sunlight
As much as I care for moonlight
It's best left for two
Wrapped in enchantments
Not in two sides of a room

So have it be now
A moment to bite my lip
And lick my tongue
Until the breath sucked
Is more present than ever dared
And all the longing for dies away

Because the truthful stab
Is everything needed, is already had
And should it be
One day a hand entwines
Let's define it as nothing
And call it a bonus of trust
That God himself is more than love.

Fleshhold

Tonight I cried
A thousand deaths
Tonight I cried
Till no breath would

My eyes they burn
My chest aches hard
My body trembles
Pass my spirit far

Love has broken
I always knew
Love has broken
My soul to you

And in this night
So damned I am
But I'll rise up
Love hands the pain

Tonight I crossed
A dark threshold
Tonight I crossed
A strong fleshhold

My eyes lose sight
My chest collects
My body tempers
Pass my spirit spent

Love unspoken
I always knew
Love unspoken
My soul to you

You pushed so cold
Within your pull
One of us the blind
One of us the fool

I reached in love
You turned in fear
One of us will regret
One of us shall pioneer

How becomes vividness
When lost to confuse
Yet nothing will prove the most
Than if love survives the drowning choke
In a rain of fire and smoke

Tonight, my eyes
Tonight, my body
Have never felt so defeated
But I repeat against my cries
Yes, I will rise
God, I will rise.

Wishful

I was a teardrop on your warm face
The faintest goodbye your lips couldn't press
The thick of the chest, I am indecent
To offer such strength not in my behold
If intrigue is your mystery
I wish you never kissed me
I might be wishful, but now I'm deceived

These circles in rain turning endless
Quicker when there's no direction
So turn, let me burn
Around pass the dizzy
I'm oblivious to fever, can you not see
Little by little the drizzle will drench
And fall to the Earth, my fever will drown

Missing, I'll never be
Roaring though rainstorms
That eat through the bone
In truth unlike you, I've already wandered
Survived all the cuts, my skin sucked them in
Little by little the entice will wear
And fall to the way, my weakness will fade

I am a whisper of every hunger
To bite back the cold and burn in a fire
Call it desire but it is my wish
For I am in wanting and scared to death
But I will leap to such great release
If I let me, be nothing
More than wishful.

Suck & Wish

Raise a glass
That sucks the light
Which comes to pass
Fill it full
Then sip the wine
The high begins

I wish to sin
Oh, wicked sin
On breath and skin

Hunt me down
Lay me down
Possess my own
Until I know
No way out
No run and hide

Bare me full
Bare me deep
Seep in every vein

In sane, in creep
Every side, in between
All to win

For the bliss
Exists the kiss
We always miss
Now can't resist

Raise a glass
Fill it full
I wish to sin.

Naked

She's naked
In silence you hear
She's naked
Sounding none but your ear
Then she moves
Into your stare

You're naked
In trembling care
You're naked
Grounding in truest fair
But you're still
Into her bare

She's complete
In coming out
She's complete
For you have found
And she moves
Just as you do

You're complete
Comprehend all
You're complete
For love walls did fall
And you move
Just as I do

Two naked
One being
Two naked
This vessel
Moving, we're moving
In us.

Quivers

It was as if the fluid of your bones
Would fever me wasteless
And I swore myself to silence
In mind, so the heart could rage fire
In surrealness I surrender
For I thought me unable before
To have what I revered

Yet leave my body and watch this scene
Naked in bare and ingesting
Every ounce of connect once missed
Strength apart, I was torment
Uncertain to be welcomed in love

If I impress lost for words
I am, and searching
But breath in heavy is all that appears
And at these quivers
Shaken to let go at the promise
This is planted
As a seed into my loins
By the extension of your bodied soul

Forgive me
This was gone to me
And death in the ground
Seemed so closed
For how can we ever conceive
Nature's insistent rapport
That roses keep beauty despite thorns.

Everlast

Lord
If thy will, be still
The quick of your run
The quiet of your tongue
Sends me to the deep of the dark

Lord
If thy will, find kind
The length of your watch
The light of your notch
No ego could win over fear

Dear Lord
If thou cares, be bare
The rich of your soul
The loose of your control
May set forth a new ever last

So, Lord
As I wish, a kiss
The force of the heat
The call of defeat
To conclude there will be only one

Lord
As I speak, give heed
The weight of my words
The grace of your return
Confess what the heart already knows

Dear Lord
As I move, do conclude
The step of my bones
The places set in stone
At my leisure thou may follow after

Lord, you cast me off
You covered my grave
Lord, you lied love
You were cowardly brave
A fool no one knew, but I never left you
For you can't, no, you can't
Ever deny my sacred kind

Lord, you pissed me off
You torched my dreams
Lord, you turned love
You took cruel extremes
A fool I once knew but god, lucky you
Oh, you can't, no, you can't
Ever be denied loves reply

As you are my Lord
And we're on knees to our will
Hear this loud, and unbound
You are mine.

olf

I'll never be naked
Just haunted in beguile
By the scent of the wolf
Who took my skin
Then wore it thick
Like I'd always be born again

I said nothing with words
I hurt the less of disguise
And then I cried apart
Cold until I died
As you gave heat to your laugh
Saying Heaven will be a find

Your piece in design
My mind crows in the dark
If walk or in run
The missing is still alien
And somehow strains
You are of everything

I'm seeing ghosts
And becoming one of them
Gripping the stem of a rose
Which stays in bloom
When soon it should have withered
Is this the gift of you?

The truth of want I said
Is out of mind and there in bed
And when I'm more than all my skin
I'll never be again
Neither naked nor so haunted.

Kingdom

Here in shadows
I lay waiting
Feeling time lost to the dark
Did I capture a thought so fleeting?
Asking more of what's too hard
This still holds me
Night enfolds me
Wrapped in tight but sensing cold

I could wed you
Should you render us together
If that's something we can do
At the stem of impossible

Disenchanted
My own upset
Praying for the time I need
There was nothing but a fearing
Pulling at a source subdued
Yes, this wavered
We were injured
If only for a time alone

I forgave this
In my surrender, didn't wander
But let you take us to the edge
The edge was wavering to me

For I was your kingdom
You came and conquered
I'm left to pick the pieces up
These walls hunger
For true protection
Cold unrest till we return
The end of kingdoms come.

Serpent Smoke

I arise the night in scent
The ease of thought
The lightest whisper
The throw of desire caught
When in royalty I knew this land
Upon the once repeat
There were wars and scars
Blood and tears in full
The danger stretched too far

Of many loved I felt disease
Of serpents full of smoke
But alas, the fall of weakened knees
Upon my words, I choked
And to my graves
The graves drew weight
The next to be redeemed
In skin as new, small in frame
The honest smile a dream

And they wavered
The queen shall have me damned
And they caved upon the fear
The love would stay the hands
They long in yearn her touch alone
The dance of bittersweet
How every tear she grieved
Said in pure, believe

The distance of a monster
One day the beauty reigns
When forgive of stains
And the confess of bare
Unites the love ingrained
Meant to last forever
Bound to change the world.

Reservoir

Was a boy to a man
Was a man locked in fear
Was a love hoped to reign
For days and days

Was a girl to a woman
Was a woman crossed by fear
Was a love faithed to burn
For days and days

The smoke became my air
As nothing comes and leaves
The sting becomes my scar
The wounded reservoir

You've been too silent, I too lenient
You've lingered too far, I've been too long
We're fighting battles we don't own
So to the test of love to be
Let us die the beast, and claim the throne

Love's Fool

How passes another night
Years have spent my eyes
I see you so clearly
Yet the fade leaves shade in memory
And each night's dream plays
Before these eyes and through this mind
At times I touch the hand I reach for
And some, I cannot see you anymore

More than you know, I love
In time I pray from me
It may show to never change
For in the vastness of time
At least it was real beauty to me
As I am the fool in the wake.

Breath

Compelled to my chamber
Led here by a curse
To exhaust every touch
Do take my breath
Astray is my slumber
Crossed chest by my hand
To tracing bare skin
Do take my breath

Denied to weakness
Made fool to a grave
Buried to the ends
Do take my breath
Fetal in stillness
The night covers me
Away go the world
So let me be

Enslave to caged passion
The moans of bereave
From darkness as lost
Is the give and receive
By your leave

As God as my witness
From hell have my rise
As sun does the dawn
What exists me fights on
Here in my chamber
Stare into sky
Tears by my river
This night.

Earth, Sea

What but is a fair river's storm
The rise of thunder as waves are torn
Crashing with fever
Rising with force
For cause to be heard
And desire to be reborn

Where wind moves ambivalent
Over valleys parallel
Once Earth had spent
Aging with seasons
Craving with bends
So longed to be seen
Purpose of evidence

Call not without passion
Heaven shall not dare
Bestowing trust, in miracles
Else embrace full our care

Does the swell of the sea entice thee?
Does the burn of the Earth invite thee?
You've traveled them
Love, travel me
Tamest not engaging beauty
Ever rare, barest barren
I barest my love as thee

Knowest a fair river's storm
Thy presence marry my shore
Knowest the wind so benevolent
Ever spent, ever kept
The body of Earth and Sea.

Rivers

So I found you first
You would've if you knew
So there's rain in my eyes
You can taste the drops clean

So I want you to come
Stand on the edge with me
So there's everything to say
In lovers conversation

Speaking, no words

As butterflies play
Play in motion slowed
Slowing wild rivers
Rivers flowing over

And you think like me
You're feeling a wide range
And here's a hollow cave
There's room to settle in

Where butterflies play
Play in motion slowed
Slowing wild rivers
Rivers flowing over

Not surprised I know you
Not surprised I know
Not surprised by you
In the truth of lovers conversation.

Exchange

Say euphoria will convene
When the seasons tire and fall
And every wetness from eyes
Shall be taken and called beautiful

How I long to be free
How I long to know no fear
It's how I long to run into bliss
And taste the burning
Of bold nature's kiss

I'm barren and cannot forget you
Lost but regaining my speed
To not be ahead yet it's turning
As I'm believing instead of dying

May there be redness deep
May there be fair in the end
May there be faith in reserve
To last the yearning
In every racing nerve

Turn to me, turn to me
Return again
I've bled it, I've said it
Now your turn

On days tide sexes the shore
The exchange builds and fills
And every whisper from heart
Shall be spoken and willed beautiful

Oh, what I live for
Oh, what I live to be
It's what I live to give and receive
Endlessly in our shiver

Turn to me, turn to me,
Turn again, return
Turn with me, turn with me
Turn, return, turn to me

Openly, honestly, utterly, passionately
Speak it, scream it, never hide from it
Let it be everything and more
Turn to me, love
It's your turn.

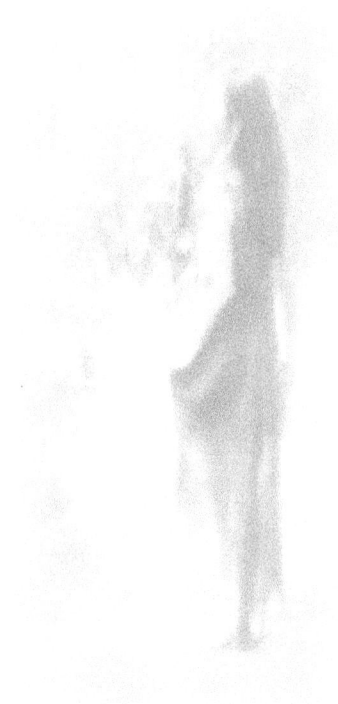

Bare Canvas

Give death with lips
I come this sin
In purity and nakedness
In dips, airs, breaths
And beads of sweat
In tears slain

I have no shame
Past storms erased
The canvas now bare of paint
In skin, warmth, touch
In voice for sake
In stares shared

I've died a thousand deaths
I've killed upon the truth
This time I'm stripped of ego
And bearing every bruise

You moved me how you wanted
Now I move us how we need
For the world to not explode
The bond is meant to feed

Wake your eyes
Bleed your heart
Shed your skin
Enflame your soul
For the only one to know
Is me and ever me.

Shot Beauty

This beauty
Shot a hole in your world
In circumstance
More than a destined merge
It's so important to see
Watch the view from in between
You never wanted anything so badly

Standing on a lift again
Still know now what you knew then
No other love for you
You try to call a hundred times
Not ready for her voice tonight
It beats you

So wander through the leaves that fall
Dream of you to have it all
Come lately
For everything you need I have
It shines through in the aftermath
Come sweetly

I'm moved by all I feel in you
Love for me, I'll call for you
Forever
And if you dare you're not enough
Turn to me, drown in our love
Completely
You will not be left behind

Now stars have brightly shone again
Stand with me upon the ledge
Fall into love
The lights were never out you see
The sign you have been found complete
Forever
Apart of you.

Underneath

As darkened skies play hide tonight
The thrill is fishing for breath
We're crawling to the unconsumed skin
For a tired taste of flesh

Could you stay to fill the void tonight?
Be the all to needed strain
We're fasting for some excess motion
To shelter in our planted frames

I want you under
Handing me out
Searching me out to no end

Why don't you push me
Wake me and take control
It's your thunder I ingest
No rest until I show you
The love that's underneath

You found me pacing
I saw you racing past yourself
You found me dreaming
I saw you feeling into me
You found me daring
I saw you staring through the glass
Asking for nothing more
Asking for nothing more than us

It's late and I'm beside your sleeping
Do not move the beauty away
We're involved beyond mortal cover
For a time could never delay

You're always under
Searching me out
The love that's underneath.

Hurricane

As flames breathe words
Burning my memory from whispers
Of waves when faith was brave
Were I to dare on embers
Fresh from fire set by intention
Would I float or choke the pain?

Come hurricane upon my skin
Blind my eyes by floods
Above my body
Above the earth
No essence suppressed by God
When mountains are meant to raise
Holy and high.

Love

If ever the sun droughts the sea
Saturate you with memories of me
If ever a desert you stand in surrounds
Feast of the love with me you have found

If ever the dark seduces your light
Illuminate you with all of mine
If ever the Earth loses her ground
Cleave to my body and never drown.

Lady Made

The lake is calm
The season's moved
Inside me still the storm goes on
Pouring when bone dry
Roaring when so parched
Excited when I feel despair
Upset when melancholy

Crowds know leave of me
The bed neglects me sleep
Nowhere finds me there
The air plays hot and cold

The days are pass
The moments haze
Outside me still the life lives on
Laughing when no cure
Voicing when so barren
Valiant when in surrender
Forceful when unyielding

Time divorces me
The house regrets the ease
Nowhere takes me there
The fair contests the less

Once more may I touch thee?
To love thy skin again
Once more may our eyes mate?
And I wed your breathful scent

This freeze shall never warm
The hope is claimed to limbo
But the love, oh, the love
Engulfs in every way
I must let it eat me whole
For an old friend
Once ago and then tomorrow
Yours because I am
A lady made of you.

Stings

Tantalizing stings
Will you diamond me
Beyond the shifts of everglow
You had to know I love
More than the earth of green at life
More than the swarm of all sea beds
As it has been said
But now by my own mouth
I'm sorry for my bite

Allowance for the pityness
With eyes cast down to ground
No matter where my footsteps led
Your steps wed mine too
More than holy prayers from sinful lips
More than words scrolled with blood
At fingertips, as heavy in my heart
And now by my confess
I'm sorry for my hide

I never lied still you saw in eyes
The racing of my veins insane
And boiling to my chest
Raged a yearn to live again in love
Reason alive in my bone
You touched a forceful breach
And the poison to my throne
Of clouded mind

If wayward leads
The sun may parch me dead
For I'll never be a victim, but a favor
In the caress of bewitching fear
As clear as horizon, mirages savor me
Unfold the dooms of passing need
They've come to set me free

Such tantalizing stings
I may give you to my part
Of tenderness that keeps me whole
The bosom of my breast.

Of A Sigh

A vital gasp to finally breathing
What was in comes crashing out
Staring intent out to sea
Where there is no sea but vast

Your silence to me, the cruelest sound
The haunted pose of the deadliest rose
A taken toll to catch a filled inhale
Found on the sail of a sigh

Bruised by time, I begged an end
I begged for the needed heal
Then poison gone
No drink of empty cups
No drink but that come love.

Same

Hands and rings
Beings being made
Two to one
The way we do tonight

Love and life
Beings being framed
From the light
The way we wear each day

In a house, in a world
You are my home
In a mouth, in a voice
You are my home.

Another Time

Transcended from another time
When she danced among the crowd
And he in all his humility
Silently longed for her
He whispered, what would it take
To change the fate of unrehearsed love?
Would the consequence be too great
In surrendering the deepest side?

And then it happened
The light slept and the moon's glow
Chose him to take her hand
Time subjected to this first glance
Never to have it's pull again

Moving into another time
When they danced among the crowd
And he in his gratefulness
Offered his love for her
He whispered, all that would be mine
Waits to know if you desire it so
Should you never request a single find
It will still be found somehow

And then it happened
The eyes wept and the answer came
To render understanding
Doubt subjected the final stance
Never to have its feel again

And she whispered, the sweetest words
And she whispered, to offer her return
And they whisper, connected forever
And they whisper, as lovers know together

And then it happened
The door closed and the soul retired
To somewhere far and in between
All the love burned in the fire
Never to hold
It's silence again.

Remains

She was one to be called
A rare seen goddess
Yet by a rope
Held captive and burned
Flames such colour
To never behold
For no longer red
But crystalline gold

And those who loved her
Mourn the missing touch
For those who pained
They speak no more
Dumb by numbing
The walk in dark
Searching her light for remains

Say she moved through your world
How she danced in midnight mystery
How she calmed your turbulent seas
How you waste in the dam of regret
For the diamond you never kept

Cry on the soft pillow
Die on the cool, hard ground
Let the darkness
Reach out her blanket
Know the weep of blood red
And vision her breath
Whisper care in your ears
The most love ever said

Rise up from your pity
Look wide with your sight
The mirage has life
Touch it with your hand
Heated by essence
The wake of the dead
Returning her light for remains

Laus partum huic diligo.

With, Without

I no longer need to cry
More heavy than my life
I'm missing the feeling of joy
At heaving laughter, lost for breath
I don't want to stare into space
Mulling over the last of past
I just long to fly and embrace
With the lover of my love at ease

I don't know where you are
Or what fills your mind or time
Does you heart rule your all
For you still have yet to fall with me
But never did I wait for a wish
I've stretched my bones too dry
And now they're ready to land
On lands somewhere from my dreams
You have been there without me
But I'll see them with or without you

My heart says one day surprise
Will find you staring into my eyes
And hunting me down to no end
Like no other, you discovered, was ever me
Who knows what my heart will decide
To leap once more or run and hide
But no reason to dwell on it now
Until you cast all aside and kind me

Perhaps you have felt me
And perhaps it unnerved you deep
It did me too, although, I did try
Across a hellish divide
That longed to kill my very life
I know you've had your demons
I pray they have deceased
And if someday you decide
I'm everything, the risk of life
I hope love will stand the test of time.

Nights Fair

Resistance made me weak
No words to flow
Unspoken, I lay spread apart
In ways unknown
On the floor and cold

I struggled in my veins
To release the cord
Affording me pain
Spread apart
With bleeds of a sword
The nights fair my mourn

Mind fields I tread
Flooded valleys I said
Drown me till I breathe
Out of you and into me
Wash desire and need free
For I cannot stay empty
I cannot stay weak

Nerve in symphonies
When turns of turns reflect
Unconscious resignation
From grips unkept
In the air suspended

I wrestled in my mind
To ease all question
Arresting my peace
Made castoff
With sores from the sun
The nights echo my mourn

Heart tears I shed
Bloody raindrops I said
Ground me till I breathe
Out of you and into me
Numb desire and need free
For I cannot stay empty
I cannot lay weak

It was my choice, I accept
But ignore not humble pleas
I gave where I believed was good
Now only give to me

A somber seed to grow in time
From a leaf to a vine to a tree
A token of the love I seek
Father, Mother, bless I ask
Love grant me loose from pain
And tight in pure, bliss attain.

Crossed

Master, I cannot forget
My readiness was not
Into the seas and thunder weeps
I was clearly wrought

Awakening dreams of bliss
I reached for one I love
Never before was love in I
Only him I did trust

Dearly see inside me
I've found the treasure lost
Mirror me beside me
I am the one we crossed

Bring again the needed skin
Beauty who homes full grace
Who homes my inner beast
And defines me face to face

Move aside beaten thorns
It matters not from him
I say with words not words
You are the only one let in

Open eyes to match your heart
Soldier winning wars
This home was awaiting you
Come in and close the door.

Citadel

Citadel
The people fell on their knees for you
I saw your light, I knew inside
Things you said would come to pass
I stayed afar from where you stood
You still took my heat

Oh, citadel
The time misspelled every storm in you
Apart of this beyond the test
Of life in these valleys
I know my part to get you through
You still move my heart

Citadel, you start to ask
Will I last for you?
I will not be long
And always strong
But I will for you

And when night came
You called to me
To fall into my halcyon dreams
As I awoke you spoke with me
A love of unbound glory

Oh, citadel, it's we who asked
What has lasted for us?
It wasn't long and always strong
But it still stands unbroken
My citadel it's you
Here I am for you.

If Sun

Pause in overcast
Say to him under the breath
She's pouring like a river bleeding
She's lighting up as if the sun

I never knew beyond this view
Say to her undressed inside
He's bracing like windstorms dancing
He's lighting up as if the sun

If it be only air
Why does it change their life?
If it be only desire
Why does it mean the world?

Stop in heart and marvel
Say you never knew existence
They're soaring like sacred wonders
They're lighting up as if the sun

Gasp to image even half a dream
Say to them within your means
They're touching like cemented fusion
They're living full as if the sun

If it be only air
Why do they be as one the same?
If it be only desire
Why have they changed their world?
Reflecting each
And lighting up
All as if the sun.

We're Still

Painted my breath on a shoulder
Married my body to thee
Weathered an ocean of wonder
Called to the one that you be

Captive and gone to a treasure
So sure no end follows me
Conversing measures in our feel
Stable in mines to behold

Grounded a voice to a whisper
Calming praise knows your face
Traveled higher in sacred planes
Never resending my prayers

And we're swimming still
And killing every pain felt before
And I'm merging through
Into you

As we're shedding skin
And finding every need happening
And I'm being moved
Into you
I'm into you.

Stillness

*Hold my breath
And close your door
Don't let the thunder in
The race has slowed
A tie is thrown
There was no way to win
But that's not me*

*What's supposed to happen
When second light fades away
A maze with cool and splendid rings
Where I silhouette your face
And brave touch one step ahead*

*When I said by confess
I never knew better
My guess still found us together
Then you spoke in deep concede
You couldn't do without me*

*I'm not nothing in drawn sheets
See us try to fit in
The smallness of stillness
Then all of this fits
And you still feel good
As I knew you would*

*So hold my breath
And close the door
Don't let the thunder in
Lay me down and rest our love
Don't let the thunder in*

You win.

Arms

*You make it hurt
So deep inside
It threatens to burn
In the stare of your eyes
Yet here I am, mesmerized
A touch from you
I could waste away
When I don't feel worthy
To be in your space
And hear your heart racing*

*The hunger grown
Feel my craving
Please take me now
I'm in need of saving
By your most beautiful grace
Forgive my weakness
Should I breakdown
It's unreachable words
Trying to be found
Through silence is my eternal vow*

*But hold me should I die
In the arms of heaven tonight
Overtaking me with love
And still not enough*

*You possess my so easily
It's hard to believe
I can lose myself in you
For you fill me whole
How can this be
Feel so strong, yet so weak
Completely taken over with you
My love in life alive.*

Lord, Lady

Master, submit to my charm
Glow as the shade of my skin
Bound as ship to the sea
The web we weave about us

Master, surrender your sword
Hold as the ground of the seed
Sound out a crowned resign
The draw we gage about us

Master, master
Companion of love
Come open

Hands in grasp
Separate lips
Breast to chest alive
The root safely enflamed

Friend, you're endless
As I am in you
Lord, for your Lady
Let master relieve

And know in the end
You shall never, never lose me.

Vessel Be

Petrified, so I resist you
Wretched mind eludes me
Now grieved, I'm bled
Pained and at the door

Electric force
Ran through my veins
Within my breast
You crept and rested
Tasting me, I tasted you
But narrowly, I released

Damning hours pass me by
As speeding cars cutting life
My skin feels numbing to the core
Penance for now
And a hellish brink without you

I was you
For the right time
You were me
It was everything
Real and never real
Oh god, I plead
Bring my soul's part back to me

Coldness burned, I knew a death
A means to see, to understand
Unto myself love must include
To home the lover forever
To taste ecstasy constantly flowing
Blissfully with me, as within you I do

Purified, this flaming river
Swells for you in seducing feet
I'm surrendered to you as to me
Found vulnerable, so delicately weak
But strong for good

Newness is the joy of breath
Yours, mine, ours
This wellness while bold
Is balanced with the rapture in red
My vessel be your bed, always
I will be in thee always
As placed among the gods
Being all and becoming more

Vis of duos in unus est nostrum diligo.

Delicate String

With heaving chests
We no longer give our freedom
Away or extend
The delicate string to hold
Step in severe light
Show forth your fair face
With no demons to shadow
Resulting to send this anger retired
Life in precious we spare
Farewell exhaust
And painful mischief
In our linger this night

Under one lunar ring
Come silver the moons
And with heavy eyes
And colours from the sky
We dance until we are red
Your crimson glow
Highlights new revolutions
From reasons you ration true
Such radical designs
Our heaving chests
Explode as stars above us
And the crust of Earth shakes
In our linger
In our linger this night.

Hope, Undressed

Purse your lips
I may bite your tongue
So dip this body low
And make my eyes close
As the night is your companion
We ready for a mated dance
But as the way you feel in hold
My soul forgets my bones

Once careful, I resign
I'm stripped full open for to see
The reflecting of the fires
Wherein I see the hunger
In your eyes for me
I never let breath go as so
Hope lost clothes long ago
If I'm to know your better
Then letter me your crave
And word you as my slave

Wrap in me, me in your all
No more keep me at the span
For wings need healing
And the lovers need revealing
Curse the light and leave down shades
We ready for the hideaway
Let's stay inside our lay

God, help the love exploded
We never had a chance
To keep back longer than allowed
As now we understand
For you, you never thought it so
Hope shed clothes long ago
If you're to know me better
Then I'll letter you my feast
And word you as my beast.

Silk of Hope

The fight of one
To be lifted and overcome
The fight is heavy
And I've grown weary
To be loved and overwhelmed

By rage of sea inside of me
No swell can calm the least
But touch of hand
A succulent tryst
Reclaims the taste of life

The Earth cries
More than I and still I bend
The torn persists
And I've raised the dead
To be loved and overwhelmed

Say nothing to me inside silence
Grant what the heart decrees
The silk tresses of hope
When the faith falls through
Reclaims a throne of beauty

I am found beautiful
He made me feel and know
It's extraordinary
A world so dark
Plays host to beams of light

Heaven
Please let me tell him
In the eyes that bore me bare
And by the reason
And by the bless
Let us rest as lovers
Always.

You

Blood on paper
Is my confession
The smear and curves
My fingers control

Mixed with emotion
The hooks catch fever
Faster than fire
My love bears no hold

I'm taken by envy
They move in all passion
Bold and embedding
They never forget

Blood on paper
The will of this heart
I'll take to our bed
When I am done

Sleeping in stillness
An angel in dreams
I'll join and resume
Beside and with you

Mirrors our vapor
Behind and ahead
I'm craving this moment
To unload the vast

Blood on paper
You've cast me in muse
Blood on paper
My explosion of you.

Bread

Beautiful nightmares
Play not once but twice plus more
In swift abandon
Salt is buried in my wounds

Worse than death
To be left alone and stoned by silence
This fever turns me cold
Huddled in the sheets of sin
Where you once laid me down
I'm drowning

Drowning from my grieving eyes
Crippled by deep love gone awry
Do I bear a cross of walls to bones
To never feel of the heart you own?

Oh, sensuous effigy
In not one but two plus body
Is sheer nostalgic
Bear me a cradle to fall down
I'm feasting

Crawling to my trine of ingest
The crest of heavy 'round my cage
Streams of fever arrow so my tender
And I'm rendered fast in wades of hell

To be separate
So long the length impounds pulsation
A detailed creation wears thin
When I drink sin of fractured twists
I mist how never the heavens may shed

Bread be the breath I desire
Bread be the flow of our blood
Bread be the forgive of weakness
As precious redemption will be.

Bodies

I may leave this body
Come night or day
When he pulls, we will meet
Waking dreams or restless sleep
Align our eyes
We view the same
Naked bodies
Naked minds
Naked souls
Upon and within
Merging and exerting
Authority in harmony
With surrender, a thunder of trust

If he leaves his body
He'll come peace with me
In silence, in sound
Be all a raptured moment
Exposed, not close
But more than together
Whole bodies
Whole minds
Whole souls
Upon and within
Gravity and ecstasy
Assertion comes chosen
A belly burning this bonding precise

I will leave my body
As you leave of yours
We shall conquer worlds
By the pure of ours
Coupled creation, two into one
The hush of it is
Is beyond that of love
So let us leave
Let us leave
Leave our bodies.

Me Be

Leave me be – a moment
The hand of time be still
Consumption of fear
Hardens my heart
My soul lonely and ill

Don't touch me – not now
There's little comfort to hold
For this undeserving soul
I turned my back on love
Cold eyes too blind to see
Is it too late for me?

For when miracles came to be
The scarred of my heart made foolish
Leaving a weight of regretful sorry

To dare think a grant
The bestowing of a second chance
So much more than I could ask
But here in the hurt
Your eyes say I deserve
A love to die all pain

Audite me, Deus, O
Nunc scio quid sit amor.

Revealed

Let me go, I cannot lead
How to me do you think it feels?
To see you fool and steal my stares
You speak of love
You'll never know of
To experience trust at the deepest hold
To know the truth and die over for
Time has revealed you
I must close the door

Let me go
I let me go
Then raised the dead

No one should taste the damned extreme
Of cruel and cold and lies combine
To see beyond what really breathes

Let me go, I cannot stay
I've resolved the hardest part
Of what had shot me in the eye
There is no regret
From my marble gaze
I braved the peer of vulnerability
Perhaps one day
You'll cross that bridge
And we will friend eternity

I let me go
The wait is over
The weight is gone
The hourglass drained

Fare me well, I give myself
For the world is mine again
The fusion of the heart and soul
Lets go and goes in peace.

Crow

Tis a crow beyond my window
Tis a rising summer's skin
In a melancholy outflow
Sing sweet the beast
Of blackness in kind

Slyly comes the message
Open wide and kiss your soul
The means by which you falter
Is for the future of your bliss

Words turn into seasons
The essence stings in rings
Around the finger wedded
To ever be redeemed

I've longed to leave you
Permanently by decree
Suppose its written more than us
To ever be at peace away

Tis a crow beyond my window
Tis a rising summer's face
In a melancholy seek and follow
Sing free the beast
Of blackness in mine

As I once was
You appear now somehow
The piercing, hypnotic stare
And the hold most feared

But here in our mirror
The waves our wings flow
Then deepened in the eye
I sly to know
I am the crow.

 Woman Venus

God in chambers
I beseech thee
The timeless maid hath fallen
To strength, in weight
From ecstacy

Painful breath exhausted
A bear of a heart at cross
As was spoken to come
And rise up again

God in chambers
I surrender full
The false ways be fallen
To fear, to disease
No more confusion

Painful mind released
Mountainous weight freed
As was chosen to come
Then rise up again

A child to woman to Venus
The Lily of the valley
Of Earth under Heaven
The gorgeous three created in seven

Wonders beyond the world
In us as a beacon
Now rested, wings expanding
Soaring in strength
So to rise.

Bare

Exposure in close quarters
Would have feared me dead
Exposure of deep waters
Used to drown me as unfed

I could run fast
Raise up mountains
Board the walls
And fuse the nails
I could hold up
Block a burst dam
Front rainstorms
But I failed

You're into me, a part of me
Time and space cannot deny
A stronger me, apart of you
We cannot lie, we cannot lie

Defenseless in shared breathing
Should have been my waste
Defenseless of mated wholeness
Once was unearthly tasting
I'm feasting now

I had died down
Closed up heavens
Bended views
And skinned the mask
I had armor
Bled behind bars
Fought the fevers
It did not last

You're into me, the whole of me
Time and space cannot deny
The fuller me, a whole in you
We cannot life, we cannot lie

We cannot be in silence
For the silence prison's need
Godly made, deserving so
Why did we hide?

I'm bare and barren
Whole but missing soul in me
I'm bare and barren
Skin and bone
Awake and unrobed
Here for only you.

Handle

Fetal, I'm on the floor
Staring lost at the closing door
Nothing is as it seems
And this waking dream will not end
No one feels guilty as I do
Or lonely as you do
For not giving way to love

And it's not okay
I miss your face and your taste
I ask you tonight
Love me in spite of when I wasn't right
Please, handle me now

Wiping pass the tears
This love always so clear and through
Weathering through the deep
This waking dream has no end
No one feels homesick as I do
Or stolen as you do
For not giving way to love

But I pray, I pray
As all you hold gave me hope
When once damaged and cold
Searching for home, I am home
When you handle me

And I'm okay
And I'll be okay
To be in your face and taste
I'll see you tonight
Loving in spite of when I wasn't right
You handle me fine.

Move

Do it again
But make it the last
I'm saying the same
Why do you ask me?
Will you lose me?
I want to be lost
I opened a tiny hole
And look what it cost me

I was not to be
You should own this
Stop coming around me
Hoping for my kiss
Do not touch me
I need to be done
The windows are closed here
I'll never be won

I do not know your name
Your face, your place
It's not for me
For you won't do
I'm caught in my own
My own is true
It never was or shall be you

I cannot begin to explain
All that I am
All I can do is move you
From my way
I am the one somebody loves
Never again to be for lust
Even when the winds have changed
I still remain

So go on your way
Find purpose tonight
Open your eyes, oh God
Open your eyes.

Past

Let me leave
Without goodbye
It's never good
The way it seems

Let me leave
Without harsh words
Bite the hurt
So it won't last past this

Let me leave
With gratitude
Of all that was
A candle burned in light

Let me leave
No grabs to hold
I need my mass
To lead me stronger now

Let me leave
I long to go
The time has come
To fight creates neglect

Let me leave
So you can leave
And open again
When seasons change

Let me leave
The rose in light
Of moon in dark
No thorn to prick

Let me leave
I shut the door
And begin again
Myself to win.

Design

Angels don't peer in my window
They're already inside my house
They calm when scared
Brave when I've torn
From things not my design
From wonders I cannot hide

Devils grab hold of my moments
Times when the strength's wearing thin
They laugh when sold
Dance when I'm cold
From things not my design
From wonders I cannot hide

Travels have taken me miles
Without moving a single step
To here, over there
Distance in shares
From things in my design
From wonders I'll never hide

Do not pull me, do not push me
Do not hate but just love me
In every weak I'll be strong
Receive me, do not leave
Do not lose but just love me
In every weak I'll be strong
In every weak, I'll be strong
In the long, long of night
For these angels.

Embed

Blushes of fate this night
The feeling remains
The staring begins
As tears fall apart

The back of the mind
Releases a wish
To open the chest
And be free of this

To reach forth inside
And grab with control
Remove every pound
Let the truth be told

From the weep of our grief
As it stings when we cry
You can only live once
But you may die twice

Let forth the body
Breathe in lucid air
The freedom, the spell
Of everlasting fair

And as it comes clean
And waters run clear
Fondle with exalt
Embed for revere

Seal up the wound
Heal us with confide
Let it open the heart
Send a gentle sigh
A heavy sigh
As life begins again.

Known

These windows
Are baring soul
Here surreal, I'm touching you
As I dared not once believe

Moonfull preys
I beseech you
Step within my breath
Diamonds maze
Sun over time and space

Above the horizon
Far out to the deep
I'll let you see me
From visions vivid
I'll let you move me

With violent ecstasy
In tenderness combine
Without our stars, we'd be denied
God, it's all I have

Faded grip on normality
But your surprise me
Mesmerized me
Paralyzed me in your hold
Color bleeds in deep

I float undone
There's no below
More than naked expose
You rose with me
And fell away with me, so godly

In beauty not in blind
But fully known, fully shown.

The Eagle

The world, her world
On fire, in flames

The world, her world
Turning while burning

So I soar

And the roar of eagle
In expanding wings
Explodes in passion
Like a suckle of love
In symphonic harmony

And power unto her own kind
For the wind can do no less
Than invite her along
Stroking her mass
In eloquent and sensual care

So I soar

Higher, lighter
Glowing in the sun

Stronger, bolder
I've just begun

As I soar.

The Coming

Mount frequent in seclude
But in limelight of my eyes
We write stories
As desires long to play
Say nothing, be silent
Let me take the whole of you

Do you know?
Can you believe?
You're so extraordinary to me
More beautiful than handsome
More gorgeous than breathtaking
A god in your own
To sit on my throne
Part of the coming of man

Air heavy in thickness
But deep where thins arise
Move slowly, thrust deeply
Desires long to mate
Lay carefree, be secure
Let me wake the whole of you

Do you feel?
Can you believe?
You're true extraordinary in me
More manly than stronger
More braver than marvelous
A god in your own
To rule on my throne
Part of the coming of man

Be it hard to understand
Then let me show
From my eyes that shine the heat
Of how it feels

To be with you, to be near you
To be inside you more than bliss

I know these beats, it overwhelms
But if together, we'll be well
Enough to savor and explore
Devour all and ache for more
And still be quenched of every ounce
We must exude the dawning truth
It's so insane and deeply real
Thank dear God, for this create
Come my King, come my King
Come you and I

Musing rapture in our merry
But serious confide
Stare our eyes, we are beaming
Desires at their base
Stay cradled, be captive
Let me make the whole of you

Do you trust?
Can you believe?
You're full extraordinary with me
More becoming than disarming
More natural than at ease
A god in your own
To right on my throne
Part of the coming of man

Yes, coming of man moves the world
So be you and believe
The dawn will embrace
Your grace as seen through my eyes.

Crimson Thrills

I visioned him in fall
Into a clear abyss
And in my reach to give
A kiss to bravely calm
Came from my lips to land
Firmly on his own

Burning intricates
Through our blood and bones
I stand to deliver
A devour of crimson thrills
And on the bridge love built
Mate passion from both roads
Catching thieves

Highlight silhouette
Vessels strong in feed
I know how the dark escapes
Into the bitter pool of tear
I know how the bite negates
Walking firm into reverie
But let me

Let me catch you
In ways long pass you dream
Let the water engulf you full
In the bosom of my stream
Where endlessly I wandered.

Fleshness

Further away comes closer everyday
The hands are no longer in reach
They move to my skin
Enfold in holds and empty all inside

In eyes are midnight dances
Were just dreams within a song
The words are succumbing to melt
When they loose over time
Meaning in choke
Tempering fall, exposed to the throw

It grows dark within
Even every sun beat
And endless petals cast
Early as they're blooming
It beasts consuming

Once that made me smile
For that sweet child left
Only a love letter to blanket the heart
So apart in all its feed

I'm miles apart from the freshness
My fleshness takes to crawl
I never saw the blindness
Till it threw me to the floor
And I began to fade
In screams of silence bold

Those dying embers
Light fires coloured less
The ashes no longer rise
Now they rest from the burn
Surround what was flame
Empty glow as prayers leave the air

Then now a figure
Glowing flickers to my eyes
The finger traces round
Weaving for a reveal
It scenes in whispers
Drawn to make me almost believe
In the sweet of hope.

She

She won't let go
She'll miss the last train
For the beauty intrigued
To see the unknown world
As she lays still
As the words replay
It's hard to control
More important things to say

This night lets in
There's time passing on
It's one left hidden
Holding open the door
As she lays still
As he lays beside
Its strangers entwined
Familiar in the truest form.

Met

Reason know no kind resistance
I'm embracing a wish
In our destined getaway
Don't think, don't be hesitant

Every distance feels its longing
It happens to such living things
Mercy, the night befall us now
Bring the comfort in our dreams

Like the way we unveil
Know the force has undressed
And we're each poverty stricken
From the depths we fell
We're reaching until
Reaching until we're met.

Endure

Could not make a stain
I left a wound
Scarring for the both of us
Myself exhumed
Gentle me, I dared not be
My being was consumed

For strangers wonder by
I make no move
Staring boldly to the sun
My part to fume
Lovers pass, but mercy me
My taming was my doom

How can you be?
I swore in war
This battlefield is mine
The bodies rise
Then leave at night
The aim for love be damned
How can you be?
I swore in vain
Behold my heart to grieve

So strong you came
Yet quickly gone
This fateful met a curse
It felt no end
Coldness again
The quest of faith it shook
How can we be?
I cursed in pain
Behold my heart was sore

I'll never be
I'll die before
I bleed without the cure
My lover
My lover, my lover, my love
Endure to win this war.

Mercy

Upon this wasted breath
I will not be a scandal
Trialed to the sore of God
Beaten, bloody, and handled
By the worse of hurt
To the end of pain
The voice resides
It calls again

Salvation hold me up
And dry my eyes

Unto this chasted breath
I will render my honour
Crippled does not stay the hand
Believed, bolder, to wander
From the darkest edge
To the birth of heart
The voice resides
The strength regains

Salvation hold me up
And embark my eyes

Until the victor's breath
I will wrestle the demon
Cradled by the grip of love
Winning, savored, and seasoned
As the ocean calms
To the ear of reign
The voice resides
In echoed refrain

Salvation hold me up
And elate my eyes

Oh Master, to never redo
The storms I have fought through
But Master, here am I, renewed
By the mercy holiness of you.

Erupted

It's just a vessel
I hunger your soul
Release all your essence
No fear and no control

To be with you and in you
Is a wholeness unknown
A taste of the Gods
Of skin, heart, and bone

To bleed on the inside
The spirit would do
If without you in life
As the spirit moves through

This long of a need
To want and to consume
Holds balance of merge
Of you, me, and truth

It's just a vessel
But an all to my all
For it's your home and mine
When you crawl as I crawl

In more than, no less
The powerful tryst is
On fire, alive, and all being
As we erupt in our exist.

High Flame

On a plain
Spread open in sun
Planted, I no longer run
Away or behind
Or inside my mind
Breathing the pulsing of truth

How can I say
Time has melted my waste
Replacing pain with create
And there's so much love
Words are not enough
But my soul entrusts it now

May somehow you encase
Your essence with fire
Rapid in high flame
Send your mind behind
Confides of your heart
And start inhaling your intrigue

So this is I, Lady
Queen of my whole world
Standing with arms as my wings
As the full engulfs me
I let it devour
Because you see
It's divinity.

GIFTS TO A BUTTERFLY

Love, Carly

www.ingramcontent.com/pod-product-compliance
Lighting Source LLC
Chambersburg PA
CBHW071353160426